Thomas Cook **pocket** guides

LYON

Your travelling companion since 1873

Written and updated by Anwer Bati

Published by Thomas Cook Publishing
A division of Thomas Cook Tour Operations Limited
Company registration no. 3772199 England
The Thomas Cook Business Park, Unit 9, Coningsby Road,
Peterborough PE3 8SB, United Kingdom
Email: books@thomascook.com, Tel: +44 (0) 1733 416477
www.thomascookpublishing.com

Produced by Cambridge Publishing Management Limited
Burr Elm Court, Main Street, Caldecote CB23 7NU
www.cambridgepm.co.uk

ISBN: 978-1-84848-373-6

© 2007, 2009 Thomas Cook Publishing
This third edition © 2011 Thomas Cook Publishing
Text © Thomas Cook Publishing
Maps © Thomas Cook Publishing/PCGraphics (UK) Limited
Transport map © Communicarta Limited

Series Editor: Karen Beaulah
Production/DTP: Steven Collins

Printed and bound in Spain by GraphyCems

Cover photography © Hemis/Alamy

CONTENTS

SYMBOLS KEY

The following symbols are used throughout this book:

ⓐ address ☏ telephone ⓦ website address 🕐 opening times
Ⓝ public transport connections ❶ important

The following symbols are used on the maps:

𝒊	information office	▨	point of interest
✈	airport	○	city
✚	hospital	○	large town
ⓒ	police station	○	small town
⬛	railway station	=	motorway
—	railway	—	main road
Ⓜ	metro	—	minor road
✝	cathedral		
❶	numbers denote featured cafés & restaurants		

Hotels and restaurants are graded by approximate price as follows:
£ budget price ££ mid-range price £££ expensive

Abbreviations used in addresses:
blvd boulevard
pl.   place (square)

▶ *The Cathédrale St-Jean and Basilique Notre-Dame*

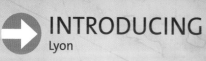

INTRODUCING
Lyon

Introduction

Lyon (sometimes spelt Lyons in English) is the capital of the
Rhône department, in east-central France, spread over an area
between the Rhône and Saône rivers. Even though it is the
third-largest city in France, it is second (to Paris) in the size of its
economy: particularly focused on textiles and chemicals, as well
as manufacturing. So it is a major business and industrial city,
as well as being an important destination for visitors, who are
attracted by its culture and lifestyle. Lyon also has a large
university (the most important outside Paris), spread over three
campuses, and many young people live there as a result.

The city is steeped in a history that stretches back to Roman
times, with a Roman theatre and amphitheatre. Vieux Lyon (the
Old Town) is one of the finest Renaissance sites of its type. But
it is also a vibrant modern city, with some fine contemporary
architecture, and major cultural attractions – in terms of both
art and performance. Lyon is perhaps the most important centre
of gastronomy in France, and the home of some of the finest
chefs in the country. So food and drink are taken very seriously,
and attract many visitors. It is well served by the transport
system, with an underground railway opened in 1978, and a
TGV station (in the Part-Dieu suburb) opened two years later.
Because of its location it is also a very good base for excursions
– particularly to Provence in the south, and the Beaujolais and
Burgundy vineyards to the north.

Lyon is divided into several distinct areas, old and new. It
has the attractions and amenities of a major city, as well as its
considerable historical heritage. On the whole, people who visit

go for the food and the culture, though there are also plenty of other activities on offer.

🔺 *Wander through the charming cobbled streets of Vieux Lyon*

When to go

CLIMATE

Winters in Lyon are cool, but rarely very cold (there are only a couple of days of snow a year), though it can be foggy with some rain. Spring and autumn are pleasant and mild, with the average maximum temperature reaching as high as 21°C (70°F), though April and October are among the rainiest months. Summers are hot and dry, but can be somewhat muggy, with occasional periods of poor air quality. The average maximum temperature in August is 27°C (81°F). Summer evenings tend to be warm. On the whole, though, spring and autumn are the best times to visit, particularly if you intend to do a lot of sightseeing.

ANNUAL EVENTS

Lyon has major cultural, sporting and trade events throughout the year. Apart from those listed below, there are also many performances. Check with the **Lyon tourist office** (❶ 04 72 77 69 69 ⓦ www.lyon-france.com) for further details.

January

Salon Sirha and Bocuse d'Or is a catering, food and hotel trade show, held on alternate, odd-numbered, years. ⓦ www.sirha.com

Voyage Musical d'Hiver 'Winter Journey' chamber music festival in the third week of Jan. Contact Salle Molière. ⓐ 20 quai de Bondy ❶ 04 72 10 38 23

March–April
Lyon-Charbonnières Car Rally Ⓦ www.asarhone.com
St-Georges Carnival Ⓦ http://dragons.st.georges.online.fr

May
Festival les Intranquilles (Literature festival) ❶ 04 78 39 10 02
Ⓦ www.lesintranquilles.net
Festival Les Nuits Sonores (Sound Nights Festival) Electronic
music performed by top artists. Ⓦ www.nuits-sonores.com

June–July
**Le Festival de Théâtre Jeune Public (Theatre Festival for Young
People)** June, alternate, odd-numbered, years. Ⓦ www.biennale-tja.fr

🔺 *Place Bellecour makes for a popular meeting place*

Nuits de Fourvière Six weeks of concert, theatre and dance performances in the old Roman theatre. ☎ 04 72 57 15 40 ⓦ www.nuits-de-fourviere.org

July–August
Tout l'Monde Dehors Free outdoor events and performances around the city.

September
Biennale International de Danse (International Dance Biennial) Alternate, even-numbered, years. ⓦ www.biennale-de-lyon.org
Biennale d'Art Contemporain (Contemporary Art Biennial) Alternate, odd-numbered, years. Both the Biennales have been going since 1991, and are major events.
ⓦ www.biennale-de-lyon.org
Festival du Cinéma Nouvelle Génération Film festival in Sept featuring inventive work by young directors.
ⓦ www.cinemanouvellegeneration.com
Vieux-Lyon Tupiniers Pottery market on the second weekend in Sept in place St-Jean.

October
Grand Lyon Film Festival Going since 2009, retrospectives of major figures (Clint Eastwood in 2009, Miloš Forman in 2010) in cinemas around town. ⓦ www.festival-lumiere.org
Lyon Marathon ⓦ www.marathondelyon.com
Salon de Automobile (Car Show) Held on alternate, odd-numbered, years. ☎ 04 72 22 33 44
ⓦ www.salonautolyon.com

November–December

Sortie du Beaujolais Nouveau (Arrival of Beaujolais Nouveau)
Held on the third Thur in Nov.

Festival de Musique Ancienne (Ancient Music Festival) Held
from late Nov to mid-Dec in the Baroque splendour of the
Chapel of the Trinity. ⓦ www.lachapelle-lyon.org

Fête des Lumières (Festival of Lights) Held early Dec (see page 12).

Christmas Market On place Carnot, near Perrache station.

PUBLIC HOLIDAYS

New Year's Day 1 Jan

Easter Monday 25 Apr 2011; 9 Apr 2012; 1 Apr 2013

Fête du Travail (Labour Day) 1 May

Victory Day (World War II) 8 May

Whit Monday 13 June 2011; 28 June 2012; 20 June 2013

Bastille Day 14 July

Assomption (Assumption) 15 Aug

Toussaint (All Saints' Day) 1 Nov

Armistice Day 11 Nov

Noël (Christmas Day) 25 Dec

On public holidays, public transport runs to Sunday schedules
(except 1 May when there is no public transport), and banks,
post offices and public buildings are closed. Many shops (but
usually not restaurants) will also be closed. Some museums may
also close or change their admission times.

The Festival of Lights

The tradition of a festival of light extends back to 1852 when the old bell tower of the former Fourvière chapel was reconstructed, and a statue of the Virgin Mary was supposed to be placed on top. The date was fixed for 8 September but work wasn't completed in time, so the ceremony was postponed to the day of the Fête of the Immaculate Conception on 8 December, with a programme of festivities and illuminations planned that night. But heavy rain fell throughout the day, and the church authorities decided to postpone the celebrations once again. The rain ceased by the evening and the Lyonnais (particularly those in the Fourvière district) celebrated by spontaneously placing candles in their windows and on their balconies – a tradition followed to this day.

As a result of this tradition, in 1989 Lyon became one of the first cities in France to institute a plan for public lighting as a deliberate policy to highlight the city's architecture. This led to the emergence of a group of creative lighting designers, such as Alain Guilhot, Roland Jéol and Pierre Marcout. Light is now used throughout Lyon at night to enhance the city's monuments, public buildings, and the contours of the rivers it lies between. In fact, Lyon is now one of the world's leading cities in its use of public lighting – so much so that the electronics firm Philips actually set up its European head office for exterior lighting near the city in 1996.

Since 2000, Lyon has taken this reputation further by instigating its famous Festival of Lights (around 8 December for four nights), during which artists and lighting designers transform the city with an array of coloured illuminations and projections. The dazzling and varied displays around town mean that the streets of Lyon throng with hundreds of thousands of people – both locals and visitors.

Lyon becomes a riot of colour during the Festival of Lights

History

Founded on the banks of the Rhône and Saône rivers, Lyon was originally a Celtic settlement. It became a Roman colony named Lugdunum in 43 BC, becoming capital of Gaul in 1 BC and a major trade centre. The Romans built on both the Fourvière and Croix-Rousse hills, and the architectural evidence of their presence can still be seen today.

The city subsequently became a centre of Christianity. The population, however, moved from Fourvière to settle along the Saône and in the St-Jean area as a result of barbarian invasions. The medieval period saw much of the population leaving the crowded St-Jean area and moving to the peninsula (the Presqu'île area). This coincided with a period of intensive building, including the abbey of St-Martin d'Ainay. However, the increasingly prosperous merchants and bankers wanted more independence from the power of the Church. They appealed to the kingdom of France, and the city became part of France in 1312.

The Hundred Years War and the Black Death in the 14th and 15th centuries led to a decline in the city's prosperity but it was flourishing again by the middle of the 15th century – with wealthy merchants, many of them Italian, moving to what is now Vieux Lyon (Old Lyon).

In 1528 François I granted local weavers the right to make cloth using gold and silver, and the silk industry, for which Lyon became so notable, came into being. Soon, Lyon became renowned across Europe for its textiles, and France's first stock exchange opened here in 1506. Lyon also became a centre for printing and literature including the presence, for a time, of Rabelais.

By the 17th century, however, there was considerable urban development, and the city centre moved to Presqu'île. By the time of the French Revolution, Lyon was the most important economic centre in France, but the upheavals of the Revolution led to the collapse of the silk industry. Many of its citizens were also killed, and parts of the city destroyed, including the numerous religious institutions on Fourvière Hill.

The textile industry was back on its feet by the early 19th century, however, and Lyon embraced the Industrial Revolution, expanding considerably in the next 100 years. The chemical and pharmaceutical industries also grew – partly as a result of research into dyes and new fabrics. The very first film was shown in Lyon in 1895.

Lyon, as a centre of the French Resistance, suffered in World War II, but from the 1950s onwards underwent further expansion and modernisation. Today, greater Lyon has a population of over two million and also houses the headquarters of Interpol. Vieux Lyon, and the surrounding area, was put on UNESCO's World Heritage List in 1998.

The city seems to be in a state of permanent development and improvement. The latest civic initiative is the regeneration of the former industrial Confluence area (where the Rhône and the Saône meet), with offices, housing, shops and restaurants. The project, started in 2006, is due to be completed in 2015. The eastern bank of the Rhône was also restored in 2007, so that it became possible to walk or cycle right by the river. Many barges with restaurants, bars and discos are now moored there, and a similar scheme is planned for the banks of the Saône.

Lifestyle

With its commercial history, it's hardly surprising that Lyon is a largely bourgeois city, where business, family, culture and a strong work ethic are central to life. But it is also on the fringes of the south of France, and life is somewhat more relaxed than in cities further north. With excellent transport links, many Lyonnais think nothing of visiting the bordering Beaujolais and Rhône vineyards, the Alps or going south for the weekend. And, because wine and gastronomy are such a feature of life, they are very discerning about eating and drinking, and basically like to enjoy themselves when not working – though you will see few people on the streets after 22.00, except at weekends.

The Lyonnais have a reputation for being polite but reserved – keeping the secrets of their city to themselves – but this is changing, particularly since more visitors started coming to the city after its UNESCO nomination. Even so, some 70 per cent of visitors come for business, rather than tourism. Because of its history of business – and the many trade fairs held here – the Lyonnais display none of the cynicism of more obvious tourist cities further south. A fair number of people speak English, particularly in hotels and restaurants. Since it is not primarily a tourist city, prices are generally reasonable.

The Lyonnais take considerable pride in their city and its history – as well as its contemporary achievements – and expect visitors to do the same. Rowdy, disrespectful or drunken behaviour is seriously frowned upon. The people of Lyon enjoy the architecture, public spaces, parks, walks and riverbanks of their city. They're also proud of their infrastructure – with its notably good public transport system – and enjoy a quality of life that's generally better than in any other major city in France. Add to that the fact that the cultural life of the city is second only to that of Paris, with major international performers appearing regularly and top-quality sporting events and festivals occurring, and you can understand why the Lyonnais are a pretty contented lot.

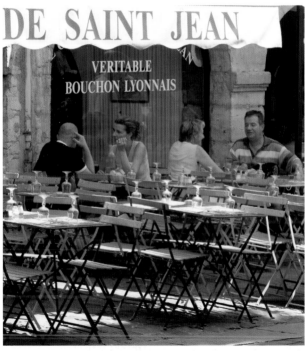

▲ The Lyonnais like nothing better than a long, leisurely lunch

Culture

After Paris, Lyon is the leading cultural centre in France. It has major museums, theatres, private galleries, and world-class events and performances.

The main art museums include the Musée des Beaux-Arts (see page 79), with a fine collection of old masters and the best collection of Impressionist works in France, other than the Musée d'Orsay in Paris. The Cité Internationale area on the left bank of the Rhône houses the **Musée d'Art Contemporain** (ⓦ www.mac-lyon.com), the contemporary art museum that is also an important site during Lyon's famous art biennial. You will find large murals around Lyon, illustrating its history. Several of these decorate the museum dedicated to the innovative local architect Tony Garnier, **Musée Urbain Tony Garnier** (ⓐ 4 rue des Serpollières ⓣ 04 78 75 16 75 ⓦ www.museeurbaintonygarnier.com).

The city's long and rich history is also reflected in many of its museums and sights. These include the Roman theatre (see page 69) and Musée de la Civilisation Gallo-Romaine (see page 67) on Fourvière Hill and the amphitheatre of Croix-Rousse (see page 92). You will also see some fine houses, among them the Musée Gadagne (see page 67) in Vieux Lyon, which is a museum evoking Lyon's history. Lyon's importance as a centre of silk production means that there is also a textile museum, Musée des Tissus (see page 81), and its skill in decorative arts is celebrated in the Musée des Arts Décoratifs (see page 81). Lyon's sombre experience of World War II is commemorated in the **Centre d'Histoire de la Résistance et de la Déportation**

(Resistance and Deportation History Centre ☎ 04 78 72 23 11 ⓦ www.chrd.lyon.fr).

Music is an important part of local cultural life, with major concerts and festivals around the city throughout the year, often attracting leading international talent. Dance, too, particularly the prestigious dance biennial, is an important feature. The Maison de la Dance is the city's leading venue. Lyon's opera house, reconstructed by celebrated architect Jean Nouvel

⬤ *One of Lyon's famous murals*

LYON CITY CARD

It's well worth getting the Lyon City Card. It gives you not only unlimited travel on all Lyon's public transport (tickets are included in the wallet), but also admission to 20 museums, as well as other concessions including admission to various events. You can buy it at the tourist office, TCL public transport offices, and at many larger hotels. It's around €20 for one day, €30 for two days and €40 for three days and is half-price for visitors under 18.

(only the façade is now left of the original building), is the most important outside Paris, with often dazzling productions. It houses both an orchestra and a resident ballet company. There is also a resident orchestra at the auditorium and the city has several theatres.

Cinema was invented in Lyon by the Lumière brothers, and it's therefore not surprising that Lyon hosts many film events, including outdoor screenings from June to September. The Institut Lumière (see page 31) is dedicated to the early history of moving pictures.

Lyon's architecture is a major cultural attraction. There are medieval and Renaissance buildings in Vieux Lyon, 18th- and 19th-century buildings in Presqu'île, and modern developments on the east bank of the Rhône, including architect Renzo Piano's Cité Internationale.

▶ *A colourful array of silk ties for sale*

MAKING THE MOST OF
Lyon

Shopping

Lyon offers some of the best, most varied and most interesting shopping in France. Given the city's history of silk and textile design and manufacture, it's not surprising that fashion and fabrics feature high on the list of shopping attractions. The most famous Lyon designers include Nathalie Chaize, Max Chaoul, Korloff, Jean-Claude Trigon and Marie Michaud. What's known as the Carré d'Or (between place Bellecour and Cordeliers) is full of major designer shops, as well as some upmarket foodstores. The 19th-century passage de l'Argue (between rue de la République and rue Édouard Herriot) is an arcade with small fashion and upmarket craft shops. The pedestrianised area, one of the biggest in Europe, in Presqu'île (around rue Victor Hugo and rue de la République) is where you will find major international chains. And the shopping centre in the Part-Dieu area (near the TGV station) has more than 200 shops, including department stores such as Galeries Lafayette.

Rue Auguste Compte, to the south of Bellecour, is the place to go for antiques, art, jewellery, fabric and interiors shops. Passage Thiaffait in Croix-Rousse is an arcade with small local designer boutiques and other attractive shops. In Vieux Lyon, traditional arts and crafts shops mingle with more touristy outlets.

For food, make your way (the C3 bus goes there) to the new covered Halles on the east bank of the Rhône (now named after Paul Bocuse) and the old Halles in rue de la Martinière. You should also head for the markets along boulevard de la Croix-Rousse, and the lively food and flower market on quai St-Antoine on the banks of the Saône, though you will also find several other smaller ones.

◆ Boulangeries *can be found all over the city*

USEFUL SHOPPING PHRASES

What time do the shops open/close?
A quelle heure ouvrent/ferment les magasins?
Ah kehlur oovr/fehrm leh mahgazhang?

How much is this?
C'est combien?
Seh combyahng?

Can I try this on?
Puis-je essayer ceci?
Pweezh ehssayeh cerssee?

My size is ...
Ma taille (clothes)/
ma pointure (shoes) est ...
*Mah tie/mah
pooahngtewr ay ...*

I'll take this one, thank you
Je prends celui-ci/celle-ci, merci
*Zher prahng serlweesi/
sehlsee, mehrsee*

There is a craft market on Sunday mornings on quai Rolland. Most markets open early in the morning and close at 13.00, though many stallholders start packing up somewhat earlier. If you want to buy wine, it's best to go to a specialist wine shop or a supermarket – unless you choose to go on a tour to one of the local vineyards, in which case you can buy direct.

Eating & drinking

Lyon is one of the greatest foodie destinations in France, with some fine gastronomic restaurants, as well as many more modest, but good, establishments. Because it is the main city in the large Rhône-Alpes region, renowned for the quality of its produce, Lyon's chefs have easy access to some of the finest ingredients in France. Indeed, they make the most of them. Chefs maintain a strong feeling for tradition as well as being inspired to be creative. Lyonnais cuisine tends to be on the hearty side, but many younger chefs are now cooking light, modern food, with the odd foreign influence.

Outside of Paris, Lyon and its surrounding area has more Michelin-starred chefs than any other part of France. This starlight started shining with Fernand Point, who was the first chef to be awarded three Michelin stars, in 1933 at La Pyramide (see page 123) in nearby Vienne. Later came local culinary hero Paul Bocuse. Today's big names still include Bocuse, but also Lacombe, Orsi, Chavent, and a new generation such as Nicolas le Bec, Christian Têtedoie, Sonia Ezsgulian, Mathieu Viannay and Philippe Gauvreau.

Apart from its gastronomic restaurants, brasseries and cafés, Lyon is also famous for its *bouchons* – small restaurants, often family-run, serving relatively simple and traditional food. The original

PRICE CATEGORIES
Average price for a three-course meal (without drinks).
A lunch or a set menu will often be cheaper.
£ up to €25 ££ €25–65 £££ over €65

bouchons, of which only a handful survive, at the foot of Croix-Rousse (see page 99), were inns that served coachmen drinks and snacks while their horses were being brushed down (*bouchonner*).

Meat is the mainstay of the Lyonnais menu, but local dishes cover a very wide range. Specialities such as sausages (including *andouillette*, the chitterling sausage; and *cervelas truffé* – truffled saveloy), tripe and other forms of offal are also local favourites (*tablier de sapeur* – breaded tripe, for instance), as is *quenelles de brochet* (pike dumplings).

Onions are widely used in cooking, as in calf's liver *à la lyonnaise*. *Galettes lyonnais* are pancakes made with potatoes and onions. *Gratin dauphinois* is the best-known potato dish of the region, baked with milk or cream and garlic. Desserts include *tarte à la lyonnaise*, with almonds. Waffles (*gauffres*) are also popular and chestnuts (*marrons*) are a feature of many desserts and other dishes. Cheeses from the region include Picadon, St-Marcellin (the most popular), Tomme de Savoie, Reblochon, Comté and Rigotte.

⬧ *Sausages are a local speciality*

THE REGION'S WINES

The local joke is that three rivers run through Lyon: the Rhône, the Saône and Beaujolais. And since Lyon is very near the vineyards of Beaujolais and the northern Rhône Valley (Côte du Rhône wines), it's unlikely that you will be served a bad glass of wine, particularly if it's red. The most famous Beaujolais wines include Brouilly, Morgon and Fleurie. Among the best of the Côte du Rhônes are Côte Rôtie, Hermitage and Saint Joseph. Coteaux du Lyonnais wines from west of Lyon consist of fruity reds, whites and rosés. You will also come across many other good wines from the Rhône-Alpes region, including Condrieu, du Bugey, du Varais and Côtes du Forez. The cheapest wines are usually served in *pots* – 46- or 50-cl bottles, rather than carafes, as in other parts of France. There are also many liqueurs from the region made from fruits and nuts. The most famous is green or (sweeter) yellow Chartreuse, made with herbs.

Although most Lyonnais prefer to have a leisurely meal, you should have no difficulty in finding crêperies and pizzerias; bakeries (*boulangeries*) and patisseries where you can find snacks such as mini-pizzas and pastries; and delicatessens where you can buy food for picnicking along the riverbanks or in one of the city's many green spaces. Lyon also has many food markets (see page 22).

Most restaurants open 12.00–14.00 or 14.30, and then 19.00 or 19.30–21.30 or 22.00. Most Lyonnais eat dinner at around 20.00. Simpler brasseries and cafés open much earlier, and close

USEFUL DINING PHRASES

I would like a table for ... people
Je voudrais une table pour ... personnes
Zher voodray ewn tabl poor ... pehrson

Waiter/waitress!
Monsieur/Mademoiselle,
s'il vous plaît!
M'sewr/madmwahzel, sylvooplay!

May I have the bill, please
L'addition, s'il vous plaît
Laddyssyawng, sylvooplay

Does it have meat in it?
Est-ce que ce plat contient
de la viande?
*Essker ser plah kontyang
der lah veeahngd?*

Where is the toilet, please?
Où sont les toilettes,
s'il vous plaît?
*Oo sawng leh twahlaitt,
sylvooplay?*

later. They are usually open all day, though many serve food only during dining hours. Some restaurants close for a couple of weeks each year, often in August or winter, so always check, particularly if you want to visit an upmarket establishment.

Service is included in French restaurants and bars. There is no need to leave a tip unless you would like to show your appreciation.

Since January 2008, smoking inside restaurants, bars and clubs in France is strictly forbidden. Some establishments have outside tables for smokers.

tgon ENTERTAINMENT & NIGHTLIFE

Entertainment & nightlife

With a large student population and many cultural venues, Lyon does better than most French provincial cities for entertainment and nightlife. For a start, there are many performances by leading international musicians and singers, whether classical or current, including rock concerts. Productions at the Opera House are of the highest quality, and apart from the Théâtre des Célestins, with its classical productions, there are several other theatres in Lyon, including the Théâtre des Ateliers in Presqu'île and the Théâtre de la Croix-Rousse. Plays are almost always in French.

The Roman theatre at Fourvière comes into its own with open-air concerts, dance and other performances during the Nuits de Fourvière (see page 10). There are also open-air events at night during Lyon's many other festivals, including films from June to September in the Roman theatre and the town's squares. Dance performances of all types are another attraction – and there is no language barrier.

Apart from bars and cafés, some of which stay open until 01.00 or later, there are also a number of discos and nightclubs in Lyon. You'll find most happening in the evening in Presqu'île and in Vieux Lyon, and also on the east bank of the Rhône, particularly in the lively area in and around the old Brotteaux railway station. Don't, however, expect a lot of action during the week: Fridays and Saturdays are when the Lyonnais stay out late.

Don't forget that walking along the riverbanks, particularly of the Saône, is a major attraction after dark.

Go to the tourist office website (w www.lyon-france.com) for event and performance listings and ticket details. Also check

⬥ *The fascinating Institut Lumière museum*

CINEMATIC HERITAGE

As the birthplace of film, Lyon has around ten cinemas in the World Heritage area, mostly in Presqu'île. The **Institut Lumière** (ⓦ www.institut-lumiere.org), a museum that traces the early history of moving pictures with interesting exhibits and videos, has cinema seasons based around directors or themes. French cinemas show either subtitled or dubbed versions of mainstream foreign films. Art-house films are almost always shown in their original languages (including English) with subtitles.

ⓦ www.lyon.fr. *Le Petit Paumé* (if you can get hold of a copy: it's only distributed once a year) has very comprehensive listings of bars and restaurants, and is free, or try its website ⓦ www.petitpaume.com. Both the book and the website are in French. Also in French is the weekly listings magazine *Lyon Poche*.

◯ *Lyon's streets come alive on weekend nights*

Sport & relaxation

Lyon has all the normal sporting facilities and relaxation possibilities you would expect from a large city.

PARTICIPATION SPORTS

Apart from walking or cycling (see page 53) around town, you will also find swimming pools including the outdoor **Centre Nautique du Rhône** (ⓐ Quai Bernard ⓣ 04 78 72 04 50). Several of the bigger hotels have pools. Check ⓦ www.lyon.fr for the one nearest to where you're staying. There are also several gyms and public tennis facilities around town. Check on the same website.

SPECTATOR SPORTS

The main sports to watch are the leading **ASVEL** basketball team in the suburb of Villeurbanne (ⓐ 451 cours Emile Zola ⓣ 04 72 14 17 13 ⓦ www.asvel.com). And of course, football, with **Olympique Lyonnais** (ⓐ Stade Garland, 350 av. Jean Jaurès ⓣ 04 72 76 76 04 ⓦ www.olweb.fr), several times French champions, and a team including international stars.

RELAXATION

There are spas dotted around Lyon, including:
Lyon Plage – the largest urban spa in Europe at the Métropole hotel, on the banks of the Saône. ⓐ 85 quai Joseph Gillet ⓣ 04 72 10 44 44 ⓦ www.lyon-plage.com
Royal Spa – on the east bank of the Rhône. ⓐ 75 cours Vitton ⓣ 04 78 89 97 74 ⓦ www.royalspa.fr

Sofitel Bellecour – the only hotel in the centre of town with a spa (but no pool). ⓐ 20 quai Gailleton ⓣ 04 72 41 20 20 ⓦ www.sofitel.com

Cruises

If you just want to have an easy time, you can always take a cruise along the Saône during the day or evening, and have lunch or dinner on board. There are several possibilities (check with the tourist office) but try:

Navig'inter leaving from 16 quai Bernard. ⓐ 13 bis quai Claude Rambaud ⓣ 04 78 42 96 81 ⓦ www.naviginter.fr ⓛ Mar–Jan

⬥ *Bicycles are perfect for a sightseeing trip around Lyon*

Accommodation

Lyon has all types of accommodation, though much of it is outside the UNESCO World Heritage area. Note that hotel accommodation is in short supply during the city's many business events and conferences, so make sure you book well in advance. New hotels are being built, but prices are relatively high for a French provincial city. Many hotels include a buffet breakfast in their rates; others charge a hefty supplement.

Unless you have booked an inclusive package, it pays to investigate thoroughly on the web. The Lyon tourist information website (ⓦ www.lyon-france.com) carries a comprehensive list of hotels, their facilities and locations, and you can book online. It also provides links to the hotels' own websites. Unlike many destinations, weekends and holidays tend to be easier and cheaper to book, as there are fewer business events. Listed below are some recommendations, but there are many more good hotels to choose from. The ratings indicate average price per double room per night. Some rooms may be more or less expensive than the ratings suggest.

HOTELS
Bayard £ Small, simple and rather offbeat, but well located.

PRICE CATEGORIES
Average price per double room per night:
£ up to €100 **££** €100–200 **£££** over €200

 23 pl. Bellecour (Presqu'île)  04 78 37 39 64
 www.hotelbayard.fr  Metro: Bellecour

Collège ££ A very unusual hotel, where the rooms are all white
and the place is decorated with items – such as desks, lockers
and textbooks – used in French schools in the 1950s and 60s.
There are several other retro items, including early 60s fridges
on each floor with free soft drinks. The bar/breakfast room
is decked out like a classroom.  5 pl. St-Paul (Vieux Lyon
& Fourvière Hill)  04 72 10 05 05  www.college-hotel.com
 Metro: Vieux Lyon

Globe et Cécil ££ A good choice, with 60 elegantly decorated
rooms (no two rooms are the same) in a hotel that's more than
a century old.  21 rue Gasparin (Presqu'île)  04 78 42 58 95
 www.globeetcecilhotel.com  Metro: Bellecour

Grand Hôtel des Terreaux ££ A hotel of character close to many
of the main sights, but not for those with mobility problems.
One of the rooms has a private terrace.  16 rue Lanterne
 04 78 27 04 10  www.grand-hotel-des-terreaux.fr
 Metro: Hôtel de Ville

Radisson Blu ££–£££ In Lyon's tallest tower, right by Part-Dieu
station, this is a good choice, particularly if you're in town for
business. It has two restaurants, and all rooms (and the bar)
have panoramic views of the city.  129 rue Servient
 04 78 63 55 00  www.radissonblu.com
 Metro: Part-Dieu

⬥ The Collège Hotel offers a unique, retro experience

Cour des Loges £££ Built around a courtyard, and housed in four buildings dating from the 14th, 16th and 17th centuries, this very stylish hotel has modern rooms, a good restaurant, a pool and an atmospheric bar. ⓐ 2–8 rue du Boeuf (Vieux Lyon & Fourvière Hill) ⓣ 04 72 77 44 44 ⓦ www.courdesloges.com Ⓝ Metro: Vieux Lyon

Le Royal £££ Extremely well located, you would never guess that this excellent hotel is owned by a chain. Refurbished in 2008, it looks and feels like a privately owned boutique hotel.
ⓐ 20 pl. Bellecour (Presqu'île) ⓣ 04 78 37 57 31
ⓦ http://lyonhotel-leroyal.com Ⓝ Metro: Bellecour

Sofitel Lyon Bellecour £££ Recently modernised, this 1960s building, with fine views of the Rhône, is the best-appointed hotel in Lyon. With an excellent gastronomic restaurant, a cheaper brasserie, a spa, a bar (with a legendary barman) and very comfortable state-of-the-art rooms. ⓐ 20 quai Gailleton ⓣ 04 72 41 20 20 ⓦ www.sofitel.com Ⓝ Metro: Bellecour

● *The stylish lobby of Villa Florentine provides a warm welcome*

La Tour Rose £££ With 12 suites decorated in silk, in homage to the local textile industry, and housed in three buildings dating from the 15th to the 18th centuries, this is one of Lyon's most extraordinary hotels, with two good restaurants and a charming, if somewhat eccentric, owner, Jacques Champion. ⓐ 22 rue du Bœuf (Vieux Lyon & Fourvière Hill) ⓣ 04 78 92 69 10 ⓦ www.latourrose.fr ⓝ Metro: Vieux Lyon

Villa Florentine £££ One of the best hotels in Lyon, with wonderful views from the exceptionally comfortable rooms, and a large pool. It was once a convent, and couldn't be better placed for Vieux Lyon and Fourvière (it's on the lower part of the hill). It also boasts one of the best restaurants in town (see page 72) and private parking. ⓐ 25 montée St-Barthélemy (Vieux Lyon & Fourvière Hill) ⓣ 04 72 56 56 56 ⓦ www.villaflorentine.com ⓝ Metro: Vieux Lyon

B&BS
Lyon has recently gained several good B&Bs. If you're looking for a B&B, try ⓦ www.bb-lyon.com, ⓦ www.gites-de-france-rhone-alpes.com and ⓦ www.lyon-france.com

HOSTEL
Auberge de Jeunesse £ On the slopes of Fourvière Hill. Double rooms from around €30–70 (singles €15–35), including breakfast. ⓐ 41–43 montée de Chemin Neuf (Vieux Lyon & Fourvière Hill) ⓣ 04 78 15 05 50 ⓦ www.hihostels.com or ⓦ www.fuaj.org ⓝ Metro: Vieux Lyon

THE BEST OF LYON

Most of the areas of Lyon and the attractions you will want to visit in the UNESCO World Heritage area are within walking distance of one another in the Presqu'île, Vieux Lyon and Fourvière districts. But the bus and metro systems are also excellent.

TOP 10 ATTRACTIONS

- **Vieux Lyon (Old Lyon)** The medieval and Renaissance area, a key part of the UNESCO site, will give you a taste of the city's rich history (see page 58).

- **Food & wine** If you don't enjoy eating and drinking, you're likely to feel left out in Lyon. At least try a *bouchon* or two, and wash down your food with a bottle of Beaujolais or Côte du Rhône (see page 25).

- **Musée des Beaux-Arts** A fine collection of Impressionist works, old masters and antiquities (see page 79).

- **The view from Fourvière Hill** Get the funicular to the top of Fourvière Hill, and enjoy the splendid views of Lyon from the grounds of the basilica (see page 63).

- **Musée des Tissus & Musée des Arts Décoratifs** You will find a rich display of fabrics in the Musée des Tissus, and your ticket also entitles you to visit the neighbouring Musée des Arts Décoratifs (see page 81).

- **Musée de la Civilisation Gallo-Romaine & Théâtre Romain** The theatre (see page 69) is immensely impressive, and the neighbouring museum will give you an idea of the grandeur of Roman civilisation in Lyon (see page 67).

- **The Festival of Lights** The city's main annual event attracts millions of people (see page 12).

- **Basilique St-Martin d'Ainay** This gem of a church is a haven of tranquillity (see page 73).

- **The Painted Walls** Lyon has several amazing painted *trompe-l'œil* walls featuring local history and characters. One of the best is in rue de la Martinière.

- **The Institut Lumière** Not in the centre of town, but easy to get to by metro. If you love cinema and its history, this is a must (see page 31).

⬇ *View over the city of Lyon*

Suggested itineraries

HALF-DAY: LYON IN A HURRY

A visit to Vieux Lyon will easily take up half a day. There's the cathedral and a couple of museums, but wandering around the atmospheric streets and admiring the buildings, maybe discovering a *traboule*, or sitting in a café or two, are as attractive an option as visiting the sights.

1 DAY: TIME TO SEE A LITTLE MORE

As well as seeing Vieux Lyon, you should also head up to Fourvière, pop into the basilica, but above all take in the view from its terrace. Then go to the Roman theatre and the Gallo-Roman museum. You should then have time to see a little of the Presqu'île area, perhaps visiting the Beaux-Arts museum.

2–3 DAYS: TIME TO SEE MUCH MORE

Spend more time in the Beaux-Arts museum, then walk around Presqu'île, possibly visiting place Bellecour and the Musée des Tissus and the Musée des Arts Décoratifs. You might also visit the nearby Basilique St-Martin d'Ainay. You should certainly walk up, or take the metro, to the airy Croix-Rousse district, if you have time, and walk along the River Saône or the Rhône.

LONGER: ENJOYING LYON TO THE FULL

Now you can really relax, enjoy a long lunch or two, and visit the left bank of the Rhône to take in the Halles if you fancy some food shopping, and both the Resistance Museum and Lumière Institute. You could also visit the Cité Internationale, its park, the

Contemporary Art museum, and the places mentioned in the
Out of Town section (see page 102).

🔺 *The Croix-Rousse district*

Something for nothing

Lyon isn't an expensive city, but there is plenty you can do that won't cost a penny. Above all, there is lots of walking: whether wandering around Presqu'île and Vieux Lyon and looking at the architecture, or the banks of the Rhône (particularly now that you can walk directly by the river's east bank) or Saône. Or you could walk up Fourvière Hill or up to Croix-Rousse. Fourvière also has several green spaces to sit in or roam around. If you visit the terrace of the basilica for the view, you can also sit outside at the Abri du Pèlerin café and picnic there, without having to order anything. And on your way down, you can sit in or stroll around the pretty Jardin de Rosaire, just below the basilica, and enjoy the roses.

The grounds of the Roman theatre (but not the Gallo-Roman Museum) are also free to visit or look at (from the roof of the museum). In Presqu'île, there are several attractive squares to sit

in or stroll around, including place des Terreaux, the place Louis Pradel, the place Bellecour and the place Carnot. Croix-Rousse also offers great views of Presqu'île and Vieux Lyon, and – although the grounds aren't open to the public – you can look at the Roman amphitheatre. All of Lyon's many fine churches are also free to visit. To the north of the city, the lovely 19th-century Tête d'Or Park, with its lake, rowing boats, zoo and botanical gardens, is also free to visit. Hiring a bike (see page 53) won't cost you anything if you return it to a stand within 30 minutes. Neither will a look at some of the city's painted walls. Then, of course, there is window-shopping, with a huge range of shops to choose from. You could mooch around one of Lyon's open-air markets (or the covered Halles) and salivate at the fine food on offer. During major festivals, you will often find free street events and performances.

● *Take a stroll along the banks of the Saône*

When it rains

It can rain quite a lot in April and October (though usually not more than a day or two at a time), but there is still plenty to do. You can always sit in a café, or have a long lunch, and many places have umbrellas for their outside tables, as well as outdoor heating. You could spend more time at the Beaux-Arts museum (see page 79), where you can easily pass a day, with a break in the café. Alternatively, go to some of the smaller or further-flung museums such as the Printing Museum (see page 80), the Lumière Institute (see page 31) and the Resistance Museum (see page 18).

CAR PARK CAPERS

In other cities, it might seem bizarre to suggest that you visit the car parks – but not in Lyon. The main ones – all designed by major French architects and artists – have classical music playing, and are like no car parks you have ever seen. The best is République, which opened in 1992 and was designed by architect Pierre Volpus and artist François Morellet. It has random lighting effects. Another interesting one is Terreaux, which was designed by Pierre Favre and features archaeological objects relating to the site on display, as well as six black granite slabs on its floors depicting the history of Lyon by Matt Mulican. The Célestins car park is a collaboration between Michel Targe, Daniel Buren and Jean-Michel Wilmotte. They are all in the Presqu'île area.

🔺 *Take refuge in one of Lyon's pleasant shopping arcades*

Since public transport is cheap, frequent and reliable, you needn't get wet by walking either, particularly if you take the metro. Lyon's excellent range of shops (including the covered arcades of passage de l'Argue and passage Thiaffait) will also provide a refuge. Or you could discover some of the *traboules* (covered passageways through the courtyards of houses) in Vieux Lyon and Croix-Rousse. Theories vary as to quite why these were built (one is that those in Vieux Lyon provided easy access to the River Saône to collect water), but they link streets, and Lyonnais use them as convenient short cuts. *Traboules* are normally marked by a bronze plaque or a lion's head symbol.

On arrival

TIME DIFFERENCE

French clocks follow Central European Time (CET). During Daylight Saving Time (end Mar–end Oct), the clocks are put ahead by one hour.

ARRIVING

By air

Lyon's **St-Exupéry airport** (ⓦ www.lyonaeroports.com) is both modern and swift to get through. It is 25 km (16 miles) outside Lyon, around 30 minutes from the city by taxi (there is a stand outside the departures area), which will cost you €35–55. The new air-conditioned Rhônexpress tramway, which opened in August 2010, links the airport with Part-Dieu station. The trams run every 15 minutes from Part-Dieu (06.00–21.00), and every 30 minutes (05.00–06.00, and 21.00–24.00). The journey takes 30 minutes. Flight information is available on board. ⓦ www.rhonexpress.fr

By rail

There are two main-line stations in Lyon itself: Part-Dieu and Perrache. Part-Dieu, in the suburb of the same name, is on the east bank of the Rhône. It is the station you are most likely to arrive at if you take the Eurostar from London and is well served by public transport. Perrache station, in Presqu'île, is an option if you change trains in Paris rather than Lille. It is much closer to Vieux Lyon, and equally well served by public transport and taxis. There is also a station at St-Exupéry airport, opened in

1994 and designed by Spanish architect Santiago Calatrava, in the shape of a giant bird's wings. ⓦ www.voyages-sncf.com for trains, ⓦ www.raileurope.co.uk for bookings from London, ⓦ www.multitud.org for details of the local transport system.

By road

You are likely to arrive on the A6, which will take you to the area near Perrache station. If you are driving from the south, the A7 will also take you to the same area. Lyon has several one-way systems, but the city is well signposted. Traffic isn't particularly

🔺 *A Lyon metro sign*

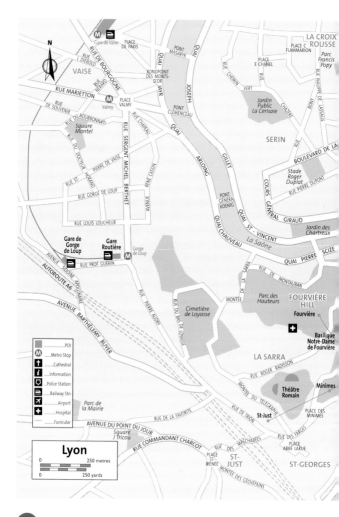

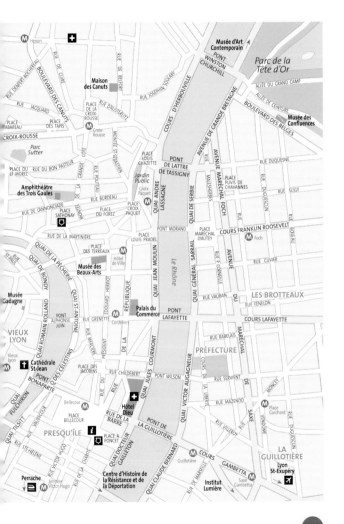

heavy, except during rush hour. But you really don't need a car in the central part of the city, as it is easier to walk or take public transport. So the best advice is to park your car at one of the public car parks (well signposted) or your hotel during your stay.

FINDING YOUR FEET

The pace and style of life in Lyon isn't very different from other European cities. The metro system is easy to navigate, though metro entrances are rather discreetly marked. Crime levels are low, but tourists are always tempting targets for some, particularly in the area around the town hall (Hôtel de Ville). You are also likely to encounter several beggars.

ORIENTATION

Lyon is a pretty easy city to find your way around, once you have noted that Presqu'île is between the Rhône and the Saône, and that Vieux Lyon and Fourvière (up the hill) are across the Saône from Presqu'île. You can easily recognise Vieux Lyon by its cathedral, and Fourvière by its basilica. There are several bridges across both the Rhône and the Saône, and roads running along both sides of the rivers. In Presqu'île, note the main squares such as place des Terreaux and place Bellecour to help you find your way.

GETTING AROUND

Lyon is particularly well served by fast, clean and frequent integrated public transport run by **TCL** (Transport en Commun Lyonnais ⓦ www.tcl.fr): whether bus (both trolley and regular), metro (four lines) or the three tram lines running into the eastern

IF YOU GET LOST, TRY ...

Do you speak English?
Parlez-vous anglais?
Pahrlay voo ahnglay?

Is this the way to ...?
C'est la bonne direction pour ...?
Seh lah bon deerekseeawng poor ...?

Can you point to it on my map?
Pouvez-vous me le montrer sur la carte?
Poovehvoo mer ler mawngtreh sewr lah kart?

suburbs. You can buy tickets at TCL offices, from machines at metro stations, on buses and trams and at many other places such as tobacconists (*tabacs*). On buses and trams insert your ticket into the machines on board, on metro platforms at the barriers. The gates open automatically at the end of your journey. Services run from 05.00 to 24.00.

Taxis are easy to find at ranks, or by hailing them on the street. Otherwise, your hotel or restaurant will call one for you. Taxis are metered and prices are reasonable.

Taxi Radio ☎ 04 72 10 86 86 ⓦ www.taxilyon.com

Although Paris likes to take the credit, Lyon was the first city to have a bike-hire scheme. The city has 4,000 hire bikes (with red back wheels) around town. The first 30 minutes are free. You simply pick up the bike at one stand and drop it at another, but have to pay by a special card at a machine in advance, which costs €3 for seven days and requires a credit card. Charges are only €1 for the first hour, then €2 per subsequent half hour.

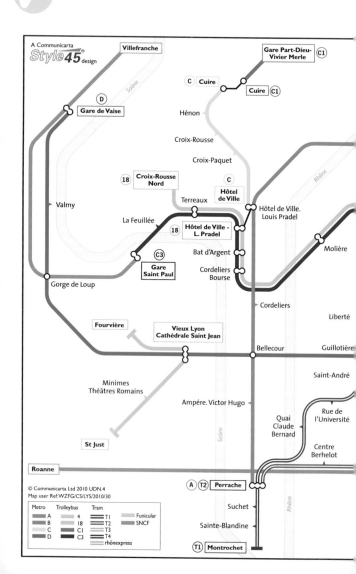

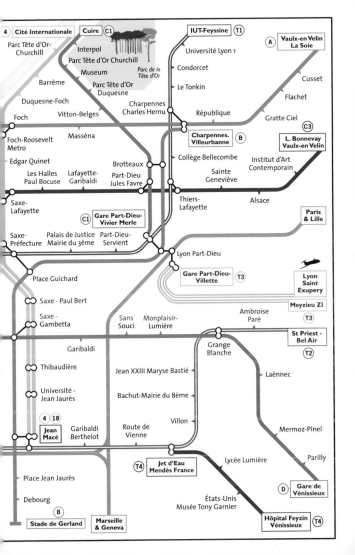

Check with the tourist office or your hotel for details of bike stands, or see Ⓦ www.velov.grandlyon.com

Lyon has also instituted the use of motorised rickshaws, or **Cyclopolitain** (Ⓣ 08 26 10 00 03 Ⓦ www.cyclopolitain.com). They accommodate two people and cost from €1 per person. These are a good way of seeing the city, and run from 11.00 to 19.00 from March to December. You get a 10 per cent reduction with a Lyon City Card.

CAR HIRE

You will only need to hire a car in Lyon if you want to go out of town. It's often cheaper to organise car hire before you leave. Prices can vary considerably from around €40 to over €100 for a Group A car for a day. At Perrache station, you will find:

Avis Ⓣ 08 20 61 16 57 or 08700 100 287 (UK) Ⓦ www.avis.fr or www.avis.co.uk

Europcar Ⓦ www.europcar.co.uk

Hertz Ⓣ 04 78 42 24 85. Also at 102 av. Jean Jaurès Ⓣ 04 72 80 76 76 Ⓦ www.hertz.co.uk

National/Citer Ⓣ 04 78 38 38 42 Ⓦ www.citer.fr

Sixt Ⓦ www.sixt.co.uk

Also at the airport:

easyCar Ⓦ www.easycar.com

▶ *The city from the banks of the Saône*

THE CITY OF
Lyon

Vieux Lyon (Old Lyon) & Fourvière Hill

Lyon's UNESCO World Heritage Site – listed in 1998 – covers an area of 500 hectares (1,235 acres). In central Lyon, it includes Vieux Lyon, Fourvière Hill and part of Presqu'île. Of all these areas, the one you are most likely to visit first is Vieux Lyon for its architecture and cobbled streets. It is one of the finest sites of its type, with over 300 houses dating from the Renaissance period.

Fourvière Hill is most easily reached by the funicular from the Vieux Lyon metro stop at the end of avenue Adolphe Max. It was once the centre of the Roman city of Lugdunum, but later housed many Catholic religious institutions (locals called it 'the praying hill' as opposed to Croix-Rousse, which was 'the working hill'). Many of these eventually became schools, which is why you will see so many children in the district.

SIGHTS & ATTRACTIONS

Vieux Lyon is technically divided into three areas: St-Paul to the north, St-Jean in the middle, and St-Georges to the south. Streets are interrupted by a number of pleasant and lively squares that run between them. If you only have a short time, stick to the St-Jean and St-Paul quarters. There are a couple of museums, the Musée Gadagne and the Musée des Miniatures et Décors de Cinéma, and the cathédrale, St-Jean, all of which you might want to visit. But above all you will want to walk (there's no other option) around the streets with their tall, often pastel-coloured, buildings and sit in one of the many restaurants and cafés to watch the world go by. Because of the fact that many wealthy Italian merchants moved into the area during the Renaissance, several of the buildings are reminiscent of those found in Italy at the time.

When you walk around, note some of the fine doors, and enter the buildings with bronze plaques outside (the text telling you their history is in English as well as French) to see their courtyards, galleries and impressive spiral stairways. Most of these buildings now contain social housing, but the deal is that visitors are allowed to look at their public areas. You can also discover the quarter's *traboules* (passageways, often with vaulted ceilings running through houses to link streets), marked in the same way. Some of them are private, but canny locals know the entry codes. It's worth getting a list of *traboules* open to the public from the tourist office. You can also go on a guided tour of *traboules*, organised by the tourist office.

SAVED FROM DESTRUCTION

It's astonishing to think that the area, now so full of visitors, once came close to being pulled down to make way for low-cost housing! By the mid-20th century, Vieux Lyon was completely rundown, and plans to demolish it emerged after World War II. But local groups protested, and it was ultimately saved by the intervention of French culture minister André Malraux in 1964. After that, the area underwent an extensive programme of restoration and revitalisation through tax incentives. In fact, parts of the Old Town are still being renovated.

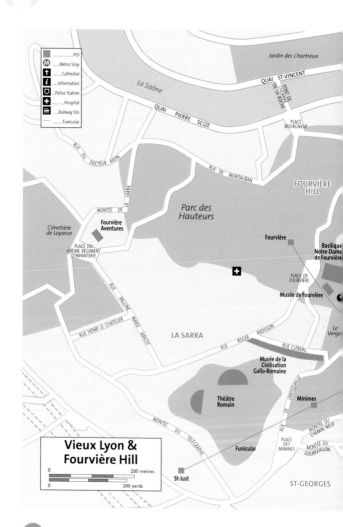

Vieux Lyon & Fourvière Hill

0 — 200 metres
0 — 200 yards

POI
Ⓜ Metro Stop
✝ Cathedral
ℹ Information
Ⓟ Police Station
✚ Hospital
Funicular

Jardin des Chartreux
QUAI ST-VINCENT
La Saône
PONT DE LA ROCHE
QUAI PIERRE SCIZE
PLACE BOURGNEUF
RUE DU DOCTEUR RAFIN
RUE DE MONTAUBAN
FOURVIÈRE HILL
MONTÉE DE LA SARRA
Parc des Hauteurs
Cimetière de Loyasse
Fourvière Aventures
Fourvière
Basilique Notre-Dame de Fourvière
PLACE DU 158ÈME RÉGIMENT D'INFANTERIE
PLACE DE FOURVIÈRE
Musée de Fourvière
RUE PAULINE MARIE JARICOT
RUE HENRI LE CHATELIER
LA SARRA
RUE ROGER RADISSON
RUE CLEBERG
Le Verge
Musée de la Civilisation Gallo-Romaine
Théâtre Romain
Minimes
RUE DE L'ANTIQUAILLE
MONTÉE DU TÉLÉGRAPHE
MONTÉE DU CHEMIN NEUF
Funicular
PLACE DES MINIMES
MONTÉE DU GOURGUILLON
St-Just
ST-GEORGES

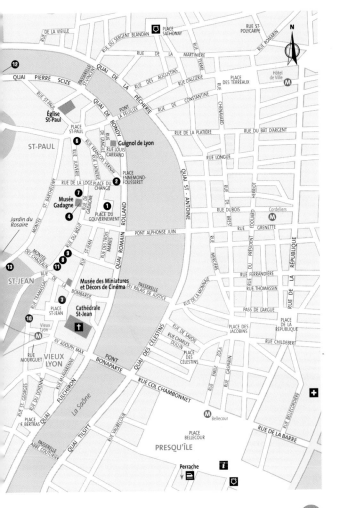

⬥ *Explore Lyon's intriguing traboules*

Fourvière Hill is a generally quiet area, but contains two major sights: the basilica, one of Lyon's main landmarks, and the Roman theatre with the adjoining Gallo-Roman museum. There is also the small Musée de Fourvière, with religious exhibits – which you might choose to skip, particularly if you are pressed for time. The funicular stop is opposite the entrance to the basilica.

Basilique Notre-Dame de Fourvière (Basilica of Fourvière)

This massive white wedding cake was completed on the site of the old Roman forum in 1896. Designed by Pierre Bossan, it was built next to a chapel that was originally constructed in the 12th century, dedicated to the Virgin Mary – patron saint of Lyon – as a result of a public subscription that was started after the Franco-Prussian War of 1870–71. It is nicknamed 'the upside down elephant' by locals. You will either love it or find the lavish decoration of the interior, including the many mosaics, somewhat overdone. You can get an even better view than the one from the crowded terrace by going to the top of the basilica's observatory tower (small charge). The Jardin de Rosaire (Rosary Garden), just below, leads down to Vieux Lyon – the route is marked by small rose-shaped plaques in the path. ⓐ 8 pl. de Fourvière ⓘ 04 78 25 86 19 ⓒ Basilica: 08.00–19.00 Mon–Sat, 12.00–19.00 Sun (June–Sept); 14.30–16.00 Wed–Sun (Apr, May & Oct) ⓝ Funicular: Fourvière

Cathédrale St-Jean (Cathedral of St John)

Built between the 12th and 15th centuries, the cathedral dominates Vieux Lyon, and can also be seen from the Saône. It gained great importance as the bishop's seat. The architecture is a mixture of

The lavish Basilique Notre-Dame de Fourvière

Romanesque (the apse and choir) and Gothic. Note the stained-glass windows (some of them in complex geometrical patterns), particularly the exquisite rose windows. Also seek out the most unusual 16th-century astronomical clock in the north transept, which chimes at 12.00, 14.00, 15.00 and 16.00. The Romanesque early 12th-century *Manécanterie* (choir school), on the right of the nave, houses a treasury of valuable objects both religious and secular. You will see that many of the statues decorating the west front of the cathedral have no heads – they were knocked off by Protestants during the Wars of Religion. ⓐ Pl. St-Jean ⓣ 04 78 92 82 29 ⓦ http://cathedrale-lyon.cef.fr ⓛ 08.00–12.00, 14.00–19.00 daily ⓝ Metro: Vieux Lyon

Fourvière Aventures

The only adventure park in Lyon, not far from the basilica, with activities for children aged four and upwards, as well as some that adults can share. ⓐ Piste de la Sarra, 3 pl. du 158ème Rgt d'Infanterie ⓣ 08 20 10 00 10 ⓦ www.fourviere-aventures.com ⓛ 13.00–17.00 Sat & Sun (Apr–June); 10.00–19.00 (July & Aug); 10.00–19.00 Sat & Sun (Sept); 13.00–18.00 Sat & Sun (Oct–mid-Nov) ⓝ Funicular: Fourvière ⓘ Admission charge

Main squares

The main squares all have lively cafés. In the place du Change is the former 16th-century financial exchange, modified in the 18th century. It became a Protestant church in 1803. Also look out for the Maison Thomassin (No 2), originally built in the 15th century by a wealthy cloth merchant. The place du Gouvernement once housed the local governor. The place St-Paul has a small church,

Église St-Paul, dating from early medieval times, but much restored over the centuries. The interior has both Romanesque and Gothic elements.

Main streets

The key streets to visit are the main street, rue St-Jean, rue du Bœuf (named because there is a statue of a bull, above eye level, in the street), rue Juiverie and rue Lainerie (where cloth merchants lived, and where there is a renovated 15th-century house at No 10). You will find the longest *traboule* in Vieux Lyon running from 54 rue St-Jean to 27 rue du Bœuf. There is an impressive gallery, designed by 16th-century local architect Philibert Delorme, in the courtyard of 8 rue Juiverie. Admire the Renaissance courtyard at No 4. This street, which has several other buildings to look at, gets its name from the fact that it was once home to the city's Jewish population, who were expelled in the 14th century. The mansions of Italian bankers later lined this street.

CULTURE

Guignol de Lyon

The young Zonzons theatre company presents productions (around an hour long) featuring Lyon's famous puppet character, Guignol, created in the early 19th century, and the French equivalent of Punch. The theatre also houses a collection of puppets. ⓐ 2 rue Louis Carrand ⓣ 04 78 28 92 57 ⓦ www.guignol-lyon.com ⓛ Performance times vary ⓝ Metro: Vieux Lyon ⓘ Admission charge

Musée de la Civilisation Gallo-Romaine (Gallo-Roman Museum)

Next to the Roman theatre (see page 69), this concrete museum, built into the side of a hill in the 1970s – designed by architect Bernard Zehrfuss – has a bunker-like appearance from the outside, and looks distinctly unpromising. But step inside, and you will find well-lit displays of Roman architecture and artefacts from Lugdunum and other sites in a most unusual space that slopes down five levels from the entrance floor. There are some fine mosaics, and views of the Roman theatre from large windows. You can also get a very good view of the theatre from the roof of the museum. ⓐ 7 rue Cléberg ⓣ 04 72 38 49 30 ⓛ 10.00–18.00 Tues–Sun (Mar–Oct); 10.00–17.00 Tues–Sun (Nov–Feb) ⓝ Funicular: Fourvière ⓘ Admission charge (except Thur)

Musée Gadagne (Gadagne Museum)

Built by the wealthy Florentine Gadagne banking family in the early 16th century, this is perhaps the most important Renaissance house in Vieux Lyon. It now contains the Museum of Lyon's history (including a section about the history of the house), and a puppet museum where you can buy joint or separate tickets. It reopened in 2009 after several years of restoration, with 39 rooms of exhibits, an attractive café and a shop. ⓐ 1 pl. du Petit Collège ⓣ 04 78 42 03 61 ⓦ www.gadagne.musees.lyon.fr ⓛ 11.00–18.30 Wed–Mon ⓝ Metro: Vieux Lyon ⓘ Admission charge (free for those under 26)

Musée des Miniatures et Décors de Cinéma (Museum of Miniatures and Film Design)

This double museum is housed in one of Vieux Lyon's most imposing buildings, a former 16th-century inn, later restored by a group of local lawyers (hence its name). The museum features a large and impressive collection of miniature models of buildings, furniture and interiors, some of them true works of art. The new section devoted to cinema features special effects models, prosthetics, sets re-created from the film *Perfume*, and many artefacts from well-known films. The short film about special effects is well worth watching. ⓐ Maison des Avocats, 60 rue St-Jean ⓣ 04 72 00 24 77 ⓦ www.mimlyon.com ⓛ 10.00–18.30 Mon–Fri, 10.00–19.00 Sat & Sun ⓝ Metro: Vieux Lyon ⓘ Admission charge

🔺 *Concerts are held at the ancient Théâtre Romain de Fourvière*

Théâtre Romain (Roman Theatre)

The Roman theatre, next to the Gallo-Roman Museum, is one of the finest and oldest of ancient Gaul, originally dating from 15 BC, and later expanded by Emperor Hadrian in the 2nd century AD. It could hold 10,000 people at one time, and is now used for concerts, particularly during the Nuits de Fourvière festival (see page 10) in June and July. It is 108 m (354 ft) in diameter and is situated next to the Odéon, a much smaller auditorium (once seating 3,000), where the Romans listened to music. You can walk around both. **ⓐ** 7 rue Cléberg **🕐** 09.00–dusk **Ⓝ** Funicular: Fourvière

RETAIL THERAPY

There are very few opportunities for shopping in Fourvière, and the shops in Vieux Lyon are mostly functional or touristy. There are, however, some good craft shops to discover as you stroll around, including:

Art-Peaux Creation Selling colourful leather goods, including shoes, handbags and belts. **ⓐ** 21 rue des Trois Maries **☎** 04 78 37 64 89 **🕐** 10.00–12.00, 14.00–19.00 Mon–Sat

Saint Jean Delices The place for local food specialities, and particularly good for sweet items. **ⓐ** 19 rue St-Jean **☎** 04 72 77 96 27 **🕐** 10.00–20.00 Tues–Sun

Soierie Saint Georges Hand-painted and printed silk, and traditionally made velvet. **ⓐ** 11 rue Mourguet **☎** 04 72 40 25 13 **🕐** 10.00–12.00, 14.00–19.00 Tues–Sat

TAKING A BREAK

Le Banana £ ❶ Get a crêpe, a salad or ice cream, and a drink, in this lively place. ⓐ 1 pl. du Gouvernement ❶ 04 72 40 94 98 🕒 12.00–late Ⓝ Metro: Vieux Lyon

Nardone £ ❷ Under a painted wall, by the Saône, this is regarded as the best ice-cream parlour in Lyon. ⓐ 3 pl. Ennemond-Fousseret ❶ 04 78 28 29 09 🕒 10.00–19.00 Tues–Sun Ⓝ Metro: Vieux Lyon

Petit Rabelais £ ❸ Right in front of the cathedral, this place serves local dishes and drinks at surprisingly reasonable prices for the location. They also have a children's menu. ⓐ 8 bis pl. St-Jean ❶ 04 78 38 18 79 🕒 12.00–13.30, 18.00–21.30 Mon–Sat Ⓝ Metro: Vieux Lyon

Café Gadagne £–££ ❹ Overlooking the attractive and peaceful garden of the Gadagne museum (on the fourth floor, amazingly), this excellent café is open to the public and you don't need a museum ticket. Both simple and substantial dishes are on offer, as well as a wide range of drinks. ⓐ 5 pl. du Petit Collège ❶ 04 78 62 34 60 🕒 Wed–Sun 10.30–18.00 Ⓝ Metro: Vieux Lyon

Le Restaurant de Fourvière £–££ ❺ You can get a full meal (local cuisine) or something lighter, and enjoy the fabulous view from the terrace. Or just go for a drink outside of dining hours. It's next to the basilica so can get full if there are tourist groups around. ⓐ 9 pl. de Fourvière ❶ 04 78 25 21 15 Ⓦ www.latassee.fr

🕐 09.00–24.00 (lunch served 12.00–14.30; dinner 19.00–22.00)

Ⓜ Funicular: Fourvière

AFTER DARK

RESTAURANTS

Le Baduila £–££ ❻ Good pizza and French dishes based on what's available from the market. Lively restaurant and bar.
ⓐ 6 pl. St-Paul ☎ 04 78 28 16 90 🕐 12.00–14.00, 19.00–22.00 Tues–Sun Ⓜ Metro: Vieux Lyon

Notre Maison £–££ ❼ Run by a husband-and-wife team, a warm *bouchon* serving hearty local specialities. You're expected to take your time over your meal as the locals do. ⓐ 2 rue de Gadagne ☎ 04 72 41 78 48 🕐 20.00–late Ⓜ Metro: Vieux Lyon

Les Adrets ££ ❽ A favourite of locals, with rustic décor and a lot of charm. The temptingly presented food makes a change from some of the local tourist traps. ⓐ 30 rue du Bœuf ☎ 04 78 38 24 30 🕐 12.00–13.30, 19.45–21.30 Mon–Fri Ⓜ Metro: Vieux Lyon

Bar de la Tour Rose ££ ❾ Have some tapas or antipasto or a drink in the stylish lounge downstairs or a more formal meal in the swish, bright brasserie upstairs. ⓐ 22 rue du Bœuf ☎ 04 78 92 69 10 Ⓦ www.latourrose.fr 🕐 19.00–23.00 Tues–Sat Ⓜ Metro: Vieux Lyon

La Mâchonnerie ££ ❿ High-quality, traditional Lyonnais food.
ⓐ 36 rue Tramassac ☎ 04 78 42 24 62 🕐 19.00–22.30 Mon–Fri, 12.00–13.30 Sat Ⓜ Metro: Vieux Lyon

Les Retrouvailles ££ ⓫ A friendly place with excellent, tasty cooking. ⓐ 38 rue du Bœuf ⓣ 04 78 42 68 84 ⓛ 19.30–22.00 Metro: Vieux Lyon

Christian Têtedoie ££–£££ ⓬ One of the most celebrated of the younger generation of Lyon chefs produces his inventive cuisine in this smart place by the Saône. ⓐ 54 quai Pierre Scize ⓣ 04 78 29 40 10 ⓛ 12.00–13.30, 19.00–23.00 Mon–Sat ⓝ Metro: Hôtel de Ville

Les Terrasses de Lyon £££ ⓭ You can eat the refined and flavourful cuisine of exceptionally talented chef Davy Tissot at the Villa Florentine hotel (see page 39) either in the luxurious restaurant or, weather permitting, on the terrace, with its great views over Lyon. ⓐ 25 montée St-Barthélemy ⓣ 04 72 56 56 56 ⓛ 12.15–15.15 Sun & Mon, 12.15–15.15, 19.30–21.15 Tues–Sat ⓝ Metro: Vieux Lyon

BARS & CLUBS

There are few evening activities in Vieux Lyon, and even fewer in Fourvière, with very little late-night action, apart from on Saturdays (but even then bars tend to close by 01.00). However, try:

Café Mode A lively student haunt. ⓐ 8 rue Mgr Lavarenne ⓣ 04 78 37 96 06 ⓛ 19.30–01.00 ⓝ Metro: Vieux Lyon

Presqu'île

Presqu'île (the name means 'Almost Island') is the peninsula between the Rhône and the Saône, and is the heart of modern Lyon. It is also a bustling administrative and commercial centre, with shops, banks, offices and restaurants at every turn.

It starts to the north with the place des Terreaux, from which the mostly pedestrianised rue de la République runs to place Bellecour, passing by place des Cordeliers, place des Jacobins and place de la République. Beyond the place Bellecour is another pedestrianised road, rue Victor Hugo, running to the place Carnot and Perrache railway station. The area between place des Terreaux and place Carnot is part of the UNESCO World Heritage Site. To cover this stretch on foot takes around 30–40 minutes. If you want to avoid the centre, you can always walk along the banks of the Rhône or Saône. Beyond Perrache station the Lyon Confluence Project, in an area formerly occupied by factories and railway yards, is being developed with planned new leisure and cultural venues, hotels, shops, houses, and the **Musée des Confluences** (Ⓦ www.museedesconfluences.fr). The museum (which is devoted to life sciences) is due to open fully in 2014. The project, as a whole, is due to be fully completed by 2015 but many places are opening earlier.

SIGHTS & ATTRACTIONS

Basilique St-Martin d'Ainay (Basilica of St-Martin d'Ainay)

This Romanesque former Benedictine abbey was built during the 11th and 12th centuries, and once wielded great power, but it

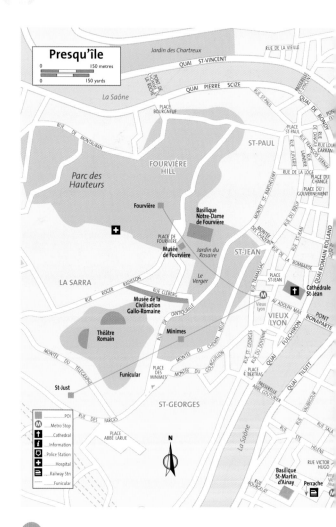

Presqu'île

0 — 150 metres
0 — 150 yards

Jardin des Chartreux

QUAI ST-VINCENT

La Saône

QUAI PIERRE SCIZE

PONT DE L'HOMME DE LA ROCHE

PASSERELLE ST-VINCENT

QUAI DE BONDY

PONT FE

RUE ST-PAUL

PLACE BOURGNEUF

RUE DE MONTAUBAN

PLACE ST-PAUL

ST-PAUL

RUE D'ANGILE VERNAY

RUE LOUI CARRAN

RUE LAINERIE

RUE JUIVERIE

RUE DE LA LOGE

PLACE DU CHANGE

Parc des Hauteurs

FOURVIÈRE HILL

MONTÉE ST-BARTHÉLEMY

PLACE DU GOUVERNEMENT

Fourvière

Basilique Notre-Dame de Fourvière

RUE DU BŒUF

RUE ST-JEAN

PLACE DE FOURVIÈRE

MONTÉE DU CHÂTEAU

Musée de Fourvière

Jardin du Rosaire

ST-JEAN

RUE DE LA BOMBARDE

QUAI ROMAIN ROLLAND

LA SARRA

RUE ROGER RADISSON

RUE CLÉBERG

Le Verger

RUE TRAMASSAC

PLACE ST-JEAN

Cathédrale St-Jean

Musée de la Civilisation Gallo-Romaine

RUE DE L'ANTIQUAILLE

Vieux Lyon

AV. ADOLPH MAX

PONT BONAPARTE

Théâtre Romain

Minimes

RUE DU CHEMIN NEUF

VIEUX LYON

RUE ST-GEORGES

RUE DE LA QUARANTAINE

QUAI FULCHIRON

MONTÉE DU TÉLÉGRAPHE

PLACE DES MINIMES

MONTÉE DU GOURGUILLON

QUAI TILSITT

Funicular

St-Just

ST-GEORGES

RUE DES FARGES

PLACE ABBÉ LARUE

La Saône

RUE SALA

RUE STE-HÉLÈNE

RUE VICTOR HUGO

RUE BOURGELAT

Basilique St-Martin d'Ainay

PASSERELLE ABBÉ COUTURIER

QUAI VAUBECOUR

PLACE F. BERTRAS

N

Perrache

POI
Metro Stop
Cathedral
Information
Police Station
Hospital
Railway Stn
Funicular

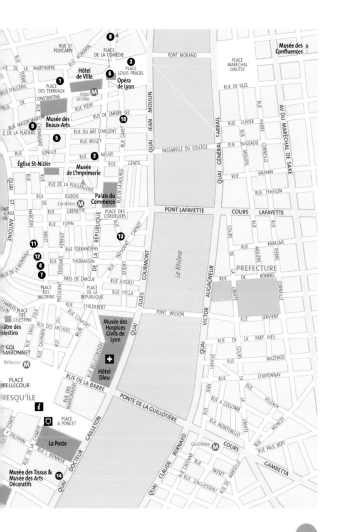

became a parish church in 1780. A palace built in the grounds of the monastery in the 14th century was destroyed in the Revolution, and the church turned into a warehouse. It reopened in 1802, and was subsequently restored later in the 19th century. The central part of the church, however, dates from the 12th century, with the chapel of St-Blandine (to the right of the apse) dating from around the 11th century. The church is one of the most attractive in the whole of Lyon, mainly for its essential simplicity. Note the decorations on the ceiling, and the striking murals. ⓐ 11 rue Bourgelat ⓘ 04 72 40 02 50 ⓦ http://abbayeainay.free.fr ⓛ 08.30–11.30, 15.00–18.30 ⓜ Metro: Ampère Victor Hugo

PLACE DES TERREAUX

The 17th-century place des Terreaux houses both the Musée des Beaux-Arts (see page 79) and the impressive Hôtel de Ville (town hall). Apart from its buildings and cafés with outdoor tables, the main feature of the square is a large fountain, installed in 1894. Featuring a chariot and four horses, it was originally designed some years earlier for Bordeaux by Bartholdi, the sculptor of the Statue of Liberty. However, it wasn't wanted by the people of Bordeaux, and so was sold to Lyon. The steam coming out of the horses' nostrils is a recent innovation. The square also has tiny modern fountains gushing up from the pavements throughout its length.

Église St-Nizier (Church of St Nizier)

In the heart of Presqu'île, and built in the 14th and 15th centuries on the site of an earlier church commemorating the Christian martyrs of Lyon, this is perhaps the finest and best-known church in Lyon, and an oustanding example of French Flamboyant Gothic architecture. The Renaissance doorway is 16th century, and the south tower 19th century. It looks particularly impressive when floodlit at night. ⓐ Pl. St-Nizier (rue Chenavard) ❶ 04 72 41 18 05 ⓦ www.saintnizier-lyon.cef.fr ❶ 10.00–19.45 Tues–Fri, 10.00–18.00 Sat & Sun ⓜ Metro: Hôtel de Ville

Opéra de Lyon (Opera House)

Behind the town hall is Lyon's famous opera house. Only the classical façade, statues of eight Muses, and part of the bar on the first floor remain from the original 19th-century building. The rest was gutted and modernised by architect Jean Nouvel, who also added a giant curved black-glass roof. The area below the roof contains dance studios and a restaurant. The interior of the building, including the auditorium, is almost entirely black. It reopened in 1993. Part of it is lit in red at night. The squares to the north side of it contain a modern fountain and sculptures. ⓐ 1 pl. de la Comédie ❶ 04 72 00 45 45 ⓦ www.opera-lyon.org ❶ Hours vary according to production being staged ⓜ Metro: Hôtel de Ville

Place Bellecour

The huge place Bellecour with its red gravel is Lyon's biggest square, measuring 310 m by 200 m (1,017 ft by 656 ft). It was once a military parade ground. In the square itself, on the southeast side, is the tourist office. The square is the scene of many events and activities during the year, and there are often marquees erected there. The equestrian statue you will see is of Louis XIV, dating from 1828 – an earlier statue of the king on the site was destroyed during the French Revolution. It is a popular meeting place, where locals converge 'under the tail of the horse'. Immediately to the east of place Bellecour is the vast main post office. If you go south from place Bellecour, you will reach the Musée des Tissus and the Musée des Arts Décoratifs (see page 81). Nearby is the beautiful basilica of St-Martin d'Ainay (see page 73). The handsome residential

● *The Opera House is a fascinating mix of classical and modern*

area around it is much quieter and more low-key than the streets north of place Bellecour.

Rue de la République

Rue de la République is full of shops, mainly chain stores. To the west of rue de la République, just before place des Cordeliers, is the Musée de l'Imprimerie (see page 80), and the church of St-Nizier (see page 77). To the east is the huge 19th-century neoclassical Palais du Commerce (Chamber of Commerce). On place des Cordeliers is the 15th-century church of St-Bonaventure. To the west of rue de la République is the pedestrianised rue Mercière, once one of the most important mercantile streets in Lyon, now full of restaurants. A small passageway, leading to the Saône, comes off it. Further along is place des Célestins, which once housed a monastery, but is now home of Lyon's celebrated belle époque Théâtre des Célestins. To the east, on the banks of the Rhône, is the Hôtel Dieu hospital. The building, with its 375-m (1,230-ft) façade and huge dome, mostly dates from the 18th century, though there was a hospital on the site several centuries earlier. The hospital also houses a museum (see page 80).

CULTURE

Musée des Beaux-Arts (Fine Arts Museum)

This is one of the finest art galleries in France, with a collection spread over 70 rooms in a 17th-century former Benedictine convent. You realise you are in for something special the minute you enter the courtyard garden and the cloisters, with sculptures by Rodin, among others. The museum's ground floor has some fine 19th- and 20th-century sculptures, while the first floor houses a high-quality collection of antiquities as well as decorative arts objects. There is a bookshop and modern café with a terrace, adorned by Raoul Dufy's huge *Le Seine, de Paris à la Mer*. The second floor houses the museum's comprehensive collection of paintings, with works by masters from around Europe such as Veronese, Rubens and Rembrandt, as well as leading French artists including David and Delacroix. For many, the highlight is the collection of Impressionist paintings. Look out for the Delubac bequest of 35 works by leading 20th-century painters including Picasso, Braque and Francis Bacon. The museum also has temporary exhibitions. ⓐ 20 pl. des Terreaux ⓣ 04 72 10 17 40 ⓦ www.mba-lyon.fr ⓛ 10.00–18.00 Sat–Thur, 10.30–18.00 Fri, closed public holidays, last entry 30 minutes before closing, some sections also closed at lunchtime ⓜ Metro: Hôtel de Ville ⓘ Admission charge

Musée des Hospices Civils de Lyon (Hospital Museum)

In the Hôtel Dieu hospital, this is a museum of the history of medicine and hospital life in Lyon from the Renaissance to the present day. ⓐ 1 pl. de l'Hôpital (entrance 61 quai Jules Courmont) ⓣ 04 72 41 30 42 ⓛ 13.00–18.00 Tues–Fri ⓜ Metro: Bellecour ⓘ Admission charge

Musée de l'Imprimerie (Printing Museum)

Housed in the magnificent 15th-century Hôtel de la Couronne, which was once Lyon's town hall. Not a must-see, but fascinating if you are interested in the history of books and printing, with some rare exhibits. It's a testimony to Lyon's importance as the city where France's first printed book was produced in 1476. ⓐ 13 rue de la Poulaillerie ⓣ 04 78 37 65 98 ⓦ www.imprimerie.lyon.fr ⓛ 09.30–12.00, 14.00–18.00 Wed–Sun ⓜ Metro: Cordeliers ⓘ Admission charge

Musée des Tissus & Musée des Arts Décoratifs (Textile Museum & Museum of Decorative Arts)

The Textile Museum is one of the highlights of Lyon, showcasing textiles in a collection spanning 2,000 years, including ancient fabrics (look particularly for the stunning Coptic cloth featuring a fish design). The collection has well-displayed exhibits from around the world, as well as covering silk-making in Lyon. There are also temporary exhibitions, including the work of major designers. The grand 18th-century building itself was the residence of Lyon's governor until the Revolution.

Housed in the Hôtel Lacroix-Laval, a mansion built in 1739, the Museum of Decorative Arts contains a collection of mainly 18th-century French furniture that is very much at home in the building, some rooms of which are fully furnished. It also houses gold- and silverware, Italian majolica from the 15th and 16th centuries, Renaissance tapestries, faience, clocks and musical instruments, including a lovely harpsichord.

Entry to both museums (joint ticket) is via the Textile Museum. ⓐ 34 rue de la Charité ⓣ 04 78 38 42 00 ⓦ www.musee-des-tissus.com ⓛ 10.00–17.30 (Textile), 10.00–12.00, 14.00–17.30 (Decorative Arts) Tues–Sun, closed Mon & public holidays ⓜ Metro: Ampère Victor Hugo ⓘ Admission charge

RETAIL THERAPY

André Claude Canova Making and selling items made of silk, cotton and wool – which can be personalised or made to order. ⓐ 26 quai St-Vincent ⓣ 04 78 39 40 40 ⓛ 09.00–12.30, 15.30–18.00 Mon–Fri

🔵 *The Musée des Tissus displays an impressive collection of textiles*

L'Atelier de Soierie A silk-printing workshop downstairs (you can watch demonstrations) with a shop upstairs selling colourful scarves, ties, handkerchiefs and shawls with imaginative designs. ⓐ 33 rue Romarin ⓣ 04 72 07 97 83 ⓛ 09.00–12.00, 14.00–19.00 Mon–Sat

Bourgeot Traiteur One of the best delicatessens in Lyon. ⓐ 20 rue de la Charité ⓣ 04 72 77 79 09 ⓛ 14.00–19.00 Mon, 09.30–19.30 Tues–Sat ⓝ Metro: Bellecour

Daum High-quality crystal and glassware. ⓐ 12 bis rue des Archers ⓣ 04 78 37 11 95 ⓛ 14.00–19.00 Mon–Sat

FNAC A branch of the famous French book and music chain. Tickets for some events are also available. ⓐ 85 rue de la République ⓣ 04 72 40 49 49 ⓛ 10.00–19.30 Mon–Sat

Marilyn Overflowing with old dolls, puppets, china, silverware and a host of other eclectic items. ⓐ 55 rue Auguste Comte ⓣ 04 72 41 88 12 ⓛ 15.00–20.00 Mon–Sat

Palomas A chocolatier and confectioner since 1917. ⓐ 2 rue Colonel Chambonnet ⓣ 04 78 37 74 60 ⓛ 09.00–12.15, 14.00–18.00 Tues–Sat

Le Printemps One of France's leading department stores, specialising in fashion, accessories, beauty products and items for the home. ⓐ 42 rue de la République ⓣ 04 72 41 29 29 ⓛ 09.30–19.00 Mon–Sat

Les Secrets du Bain A lovely little shop selling perfumes and soaps that transform the basic wash and brush-up into an exercise in

⬤ *Treat yourself to fine Lyonnais silk from L'Atelier de Soierie*

luxurious self-indulgence. ⓐ 47 rue Franklin, off rue Victor Hugo
🕿 04 78 38 39 57 🕓 09.00–18.30 Tues–Sat

Sophie Guyot Clothing, jewellery and accessories by this prize-winning local designer. ⓐ Rue St-Polycarpe 🕿 04 72 07 79 60
🕓 14.00–19.00 Mon–Fri

TAKING A BREAK

Café Leffe £ ❶ Sit outside and enjoy a plate of mussels and chips, or a salad. ⓐ 1 pl. des Terreaux 🕿 04 78 27 27 07
🕓 09.00–18.00 Ⓜ Metro: Hôtel de Ville

L'Harmonie des Vins £ ❷ As the name suggests, wine is the thing here, with snacks and more to accompany it. ⓐ 9 rue Neuve 🕿 04 72 98 85 59 Ⓦ www.harmoniedesvins.fr
🕓 10.00–01.00 Tues–Sat Ⓜ Metro: Hôtel de Ville

Les Arcades £–££ ❸ Just to one side of the opera house, this bar and brasserie (and its terrace) attracts custom all day long. Try one of the huge salads, a traditional dish or some of their oriental offerings. ❸ 15 pl. Louis Pradel ❶ 04 78 30 19 80 ❷ 11.00–24.00 (last orders for food 22.00); 06.00–03.00 (bar) ❷ Metro: Hôtel de Ville

Winch £–££ ❹ A wood-panelled interior with a nautical theme plus outdoor seating. You can get a salad, an omelette or something more substantial. ❸ 62 rue Mercière ❶ 04 78 37 23 65 ❷ 12.00–13.30, 20.00–21.30 Mon–Sat ❷ Metro: Cordeliers

Léon de Lyon ££ ❺ This brasserie with impeccable service used to have two Michelin stars, but chef Jean-Pierre Lacombe decided to simplify his cuisine, so the food is now much more affordable in this local institution, which has been going since 1904. ❸ 1 rue Pléney ❶ 04 72 10 11 12 ❷ www.leondelyon.com ❷ 12.00–14.30, 19.00–23.00 ❷ Metro: Cordeliers

Les Muses de l'Opéra ££ ❻ In the glass roof of the opera house, with splendid views of Lyon. Serving a mixture of modern, traditional and international dishes. ❸ 1 pl. de la Comédie ❶ 04 72 00 45 58 ❷ 12.00–14.00, 20.00–22.00 Mon–Sat ❷ Metro: Hôtel de Ville

AFTER DARK

RESTAURANTS

Le Bistrot de Lyon ££ ❼ A busy, traditional brasserie (with tables outside) dating from 1896, with belle époque décor. Good fish

and seafood, as well as meat. 64 rue Mercière
04 78 38 47 47 12.00–14.30 Mon–Thur, 12.00–14.30,
19.00–24.00 Fri & Sat, 12.00–14.30, 19.00–23.00 Sun
Metro: Cordeliers

Bonâme de Bruno ££ The menu changes daily in this
restaurant run by Bruno Didierlaurent, once a colleague of
Bruno Loubet in London. The accomplished and creative dishes
are based on high-quality ingredients, with some unusual
combinations. The atmosphere is warm, and the lunch menu,
in particular, very good value. 5 grande rue des Feuillants
04 78 30 83 93 www.restaurant-labonamedebruno.com
12.00–14.00 Tues–Fri, 20.00–24.00 Sat (best to book if you
want to eat after 22.00) Metro: Hôtel de Ville

Café des Fédérations ££ One of Lyon's best-known *bouchons*,
with a jolly atmosphere and local cuisine. 10 rue Major-Martin
04 78 28 26 00 12.00–14.00, 18.00–21.30 Metro: Hôtel de Ville

Chez Georges ££ This is one of the best *bouchons* in Lyon (it's
small and always packed), serving generous portions of typical
Lyonnais food – that you are expected to finish. 8 rue Garet
04 78 28 30 46 12.00–14.00, 19.30–22.00 Mon–Fri,
12.00–14.00, 19.30–23.00 Sat Metro: Hôtel de Ville

Gaston ££ Designed around a farmhouse theme (also tables
outside), go for the big portions of excellent grills and roasts, served
with dauphinois potatoes or chips. Friendly service. 41 rue
Mercière 04 72 41 87 86 12.00–23.30 Metro: Cordeliers

Mercière ££ ⑫ Choose from traditional dishes such as coq au vin, Lyonnais specialities or more eclectic offerings. The set menus are very good value. ⓐ 56 rue Mercière ⓣ 04 78 37 67 35 ⓛ 12.00–14.15, 19.00–23.00 ⓜ Metro: Cordeliers

Le Bec & Taka £££ ⑬ One of Lyon's most celebrated young chefs serves inventive modern food with oriental influences in a formal setting. Le Bec's latest venture (which opened in 2010) is Rue Le Bec, a vast restaurant, shop and bar complex – with a terrace by the river, and a garden – in the new Confluence area. The menu there is cheaper and extensive, using the finest ingredients. Not easy to get to, but packed full of fashionable locals. Le Bec & Taka ⓐ 14 rue Grôlée ⓣ 04 78 42 15 35 ⓛ 12.00–14.00, 19.30–21.30 Tues–Sat (last orders 09.30) ⓜ Metro: Cordeliers. Rue Le Bec ⓐ 43 quai Rambaud ⓣ 04 78 92 87 87 ⓦ www.nicholaslebec.com ⓛ Mon–Sat, and Sun lunch

Les Trois Dômes £££ ⑭ Situated at the top of the Sofitel hotel, with panoramic views over the Rhône and Presqu'île, this is one of Lyon's best restaurants. Alain Desvilles' cooking is delicious, light and beautifully presented. The service is immaculate, and the atmosphere is pleasant and relaxed. ⓐ 20 quai Gailleton ⓣ 04 72 41 20 97 ⓦ www.les-3-domes.com ⓛ 12.00–13.45, 19.30–21.45 Tues–Sat (Mar–late July & Sept–Jan) ⓜ Metro: Bellecour

BARS & CLUBS

L'Ambassade A small but very lively nightclub. ⓐ 4 rue Stella ⓣ 04 78 42 23 23 ⓛ 23.00–05.00 Wed–Sat ⓜ Metro: Cordeliers

Le Comptoir de la Bourse A smart and extremely popular cocktail bar. ⓐ 33 rue de la Bourse ⓣ 04 72 41 71 52 ⓛ 19.30–03.00 Mon–Sat ⓝ Metro: Cordeliers

Palais de la Bière A wood-panelled beer bar, with a wide selection to choose from. ⓐ 1 rue Terme ⓣ 04 78 27 94 00 ⓛ 18.00–02.00 Tues–Sat ⓝ Metro: Hôtel de Ville

Le Voxx A hip bar by the Saône, with a terrace. ⓐ 1 rue d'Algérie ⓣ 04 78 28 33 87 ⓛ 08.00–03.00 Mon–Fri, 10.00–03.00 Sat & Sun ⓝ Metro: Hôtel de Ville

PERFORMANCE ARTS

Opéra National de Lyon The opera house mounts impressive major productions of international quality. You may need to book ahead. ⓐ 1 pl. de la Comédie ⓣ 04 72 00 45 45 ⓦ www.opera-lyon.org ⓛ Hours vary according to production being staged ⓝ Metro: Hôtel de Ville

Théâtre des Célestins Lyon's main theatre, in a magnificent building, with a classical repertoire. ⓐ 4 rue Charles Dullin ⓣ 04 72 77 40 00 ⓦ www.celestins-lyon.org ⓛ Hours vary according to production being staged ⓝ Metro: Bellecour

Croix-Rousse

The essentially residential Croix-Rousse quarter has a village-like atmosphere, and is much loved by its inhabitants, who see themselves as Croix-Roussien first and Lyonnais second. It is a mixed area, with residents in different income brackets, including Algerian immigrants. As one of Lyon's most pleasant areas, it is being gentrified – though some of it is still rundown – and has become a favourite with 'Bo-Bos' (*bourgeois-bohèmes*), well-off arty types. The name of the area, meaning 'Russet Cross', refers to a stone cross that stood here before the Revolution.

The slopes of Croix-Rousse, but not the plateau above, are part of the UNESCO World Heritage Site, but there are very few formal sites to visit. Instead, go for the relaxed atmosphere, and the views of the rest of Lyon. You probably won't spend more than half a day here. You can reach Croix-Rousse from Presqu'île by walking uphill (there are several sets of steps that will take you to the top of the hill) or take the metro (to Croix-Rousse).

Head directly south from Croix-Rousse metro station to the end of rue des Pierres Plantées for outstanding views of Vieux Lyon and Fourvière. Next to the viewing point is a small park, and steps leading down the hill. There are also several other viewing points in Croix-Rousse.

If you decide to walk up (or down) the hill, try to visit the charming place Sathonay, with its boule pitch, fountains and fashionable cafés – one of the most pleasant squares in Lyon.

Croix-Rousse

SIGHTS & ATTRACTIONS

Amphithéâtre des Trois Gaules (Three Gaules Amphitheatre)

Unearthed in 1954, and probably built in AD 19 for gladiatorial combat, and other violent games, many an early Christian met their death here. Though you can't actually visit the site itself, which has still to be fully excavated, you can look at it from montée des Carmélites and rue Sportisse.

Boulevard de la Croix-Rousse

Leading off place de la Croix-Rousse is boulevard de la Croix-Rousse, with its colourful morning food market (except Monday). The square and the boulevard are the scene of a funfair, la Vogue, held in autumn, from October to mid-November. Roasted chestnuts are a feature of the festivities. Running north from boulevard de

---

TALL ORDER

Once 'the working hill' as opposed to 'the praying hill' (Fourvière), Croix-Rousse developed as it is today in the early 19th century because of the invention of the Jacquard silk loom, which was too big for the buildings in Vieux Lyon. As a result, most of the unadorned tall buildings in Croix-Rousse, with their high windows, sprang up to house silk looms and weavers – who also lived in them. Naturally, today these five-storey buildings, with their lofty oak-beamed interiors (the silk looms were attached to the beams), have been converted into much-sought-after apartments.

⬥ *The houses of Croix-Rousse looking out over Lyon*

la Croix-Rousse is another main street full of shops, boulevard des Canuts. Go up here to the junction of rue Denfert-Rochereau and you will find one of Lyon's best *trompe-l'œil* painted walls. It is also the largest, first created in 1987 but repainted in 1997.

Église St-Bruno (Church of St Bruno)

Designed (apart from its 19th-century façade) by local architect Ferdinand Delamonce, this is Lyon's only Baroque church. It was built on the site of an old Carthusian monastery in the 18th century. The canopy is by Soufflet, who also designed the dome of the Hôtel Dieu hospital, and several other buildings in Lyon. There are occasional concerts of music suitable to the venue – check with the tourist office. ❸ Rue Pierre Dupont (near rue des Chartreux) ◐ 15.00–17.00 Mon–Sat, closed Sun & public holidays

Joseph-Marie Jacquard, inventor of the silk loom

Traboules

Croix-Rousse also has many *traboules* (marked by a lion's head symbol) that go north–south and are used by locals as short cuts to and from Presqu'île. *Traboule* routes are indicated by arrows next to the lion's head symbols. One of the most interesting leads from the cour des Voraces. The courtyard and its huge stairway, which looks like it's made of concrete but is in fact stone, gets its name from Canuts (see box below) who rebelled in the 19th century. According to legend the Voraces (voracious ones) protested when the size of a pot of wine was reduced

SILK WEAVERS

The main square is place de la Croix-Rousse, in which there is a statue of Joseph-Marie Jacquard, inventor of the loom bearing his name. He designed the machine in the early 19th century. With its perforated card system, it made weaving complex designs much easier, but also led to a cutback in the number of weavers that were needed. As a result, the Canuts (silk weavers) rebelled several times in the early 19th century, because of unemployment and poor wages. Eventually some of the silk workshops moved out of Lyon, and later, silkworm disease, the loss of foreign markets and the development of synthetic fabrics in the early 20th century, meant that silk-weaving gradually disappeared from Lyon almost entirely. Only a few high-quality operations remain, mostly restoring old silk or catering for leading fashion houses.

from 1 litre to 46 cl – a size still used today throughout Lyon. There are several ways into the *traboule*: 9 place Colbert (accessible from boulevard de la Croix-Rousse), 14 bis montée St-Sébastien and 29 rue Imbert Colomès. The *traboules* of Lyon generally, but those in Croix-Rousse in particular, were very important to the French Resistance in Lyon during World War II. The movement was led locally by Jean Moulin (he was later tortured by the Germans, and died in 1943), whose base was in Croix-Rousse.

CULTURE

Maison des Canuts (House of the Silk Weavers)

The 45-minute guided tours at this museum take you through the history of silk and how it was woven on hand looms – with demonstrations – as well as how silk weavers lived. The museum is also an active workshop, restoring old silk. There is a shop across the road (where you buy your ticket) that sells silk scarves, ties and fabrics. Although there are only two guided visits a day, you can always pop into the shop, where old looms are also kept, and ask if you can look at the workshop. ⓐ 10 rue d'Ivry ❶ 04 78 28 62 04 ⓦ www.maisondescanuts.com ❷ 10.00–18.30 Tues–Sat, guided tours: 11.00 and 15.30, closed Sun, Mon, public holidays & first week in Jan ❶ Admission charge

RETAIL THERAPY

As a residential area, Croix-Rousse doesn't have much more to drain your wallet or handbag than everyday shops. But there is

○ *Admire the old silk looms at the Maison des Canuts*

⬥ Shops lined up along passage Thiaffait

a food market, with over 100 stallholders, on boulevard de la Croix-Rousse from 06.00 to 12.30 Tues–Sun. You should also try the covered passage **Thiaffait** (ⓦ www.villagedescreateurs.fr), on the slopes of the hill, with fashion and other designer shops. There's also the Maison des Canuts (see page 96).

TAKING A BREAK

Le Canut et les Gones £–££ ❶ A *bouchon* concentrating on fresh, local produce. ⓐ 29 rue de Belfort ⓣ 04 78 29 17 23 ⓛ 12.00–14.00, 20.00–23.00 Tues–Sat Ⓜ Metro: Croix-Rousse

Le Canut Sans Cervelle £–££ ❷ With a patio, serving traditional cuisine and well known for Sunday brunch from Sept to May. Good value at lunchtime. ⓐ 4 bis rue de Belfort ⓣ 04 78 30 10 20 ⓛ 12.00–14.00, 19.30–22.30 Sun–Tues, Thur & Fri, 12.00–14.00 Sat Ⓜ Metro: Croix-Rousse

La Famille £–££ ❸ A friendly family-run place, serving generous portions of filling comfort food at decent prices, particularly at lunchtime. ⓐ 18 rue Duviard, off rue Perrod ⓣ 04 72 98 83 90 ⓛ 12.00–14.00, 19.30–22.30 Tues–Sat Ⓜ Metro: Croix-Rousse

AFTER DARK

RESTAURANTS
Comptoir du Mail £–££ ❹ A favourite with locals, you can get a simple snack or a more intricate dinner. ⓐ 14 rue du Mail

☎ 04 78 27 71 40 🕐 12.00–13.45, 19.00–21.45 Tues–Sat
Ⓜ Metro: Croix-Rousse

Maison Villemanzy £–££ ❺ In a house on the slopes of Croix-Rousse, with a terrace offering fine views and tempting food that's cooked to a high standard. 🅐 25 montée St-Sébastien ☎ 04 72 98 21 21 🕐 19.30–22.00 Mon, 12.00–14.00, 19.30–22.00 Tues–Sat Ⓜ Metro: Croix-Paquet

Le Plato £–££ ❻ Seasonal market cuisine, with some unusual twists (duck breast with coriander, for instance). Also a very good wine list. 🅐 1 rue Villeneuve ☎ 04 72 00 01 30 🆆 www.leplato.com 🕐 12.00–14.30, 19.30–23.30 Mon–Sat Ⓜ Metro: Croix-Rousse

BARS & CLUBS
There isn't much late-night activity in Croix-Rousse, but you could try:

Modern Art Café A bar displaying contemporary art, with a DJ in the evening and good cocktails. You can also eat light dishes, and go for brunch (11.00–15.00) on Sundays. You can sit outside in good weather. 🅐 65 blvd de la Croix-Rousse ☎ 04 72 87 06 82 🆆 www.modernartcafe.net 🕐 11.30–02.00 daily (summer); 17.00–02.00 daily (winter) Ⓜ Metro: Croix-Rousse

▶ *Vienne's Roman temple*

OUT OF TOWN
trips

Pérouges

The small hill village of Pérouges, built between the 12th and 15th centuries, is officially designated as one of the most beautiful in France, and would make a good half-day trip as a contrast to the bustle of Lyon. The hill was once the site of a Roman watchtower, and legend has it that the village was founded by a tribe of Gauls from Perugia in Italy (hence its name). Whether or not this is true, a castle was built on the hill in the 12th century, and the site was fortified. Pérouges has changed hands many times during its long history. It was once Dauphinois, and in 1345 came under the rule of the Dukes of Savoy. It eventually became French in 1601. It was during its Savoyard period that Pérouges had its finest hour, withstanding a siege by the Dauphinois in 1468. The part of the village that was then outside the fortifications was, however, destroyed, and the inhabitants then moved to the top of the hill, within the ramparts. Pérouges was known as a centre of crafts, in particular the weaving of hemp cloth. It is a charming and peaceful place, with some excellent views, interesting shops and decent restaurants.

GETTING THERE

The best way to get to Pérouges, which is 34 km (21 miles) northeast of Lyon, is to take a train from Part-Dieu or Perrache station to Méximieux-Pérouges (30–50 minutes, depending on the train). Alternatively, drive via the A6/E15 and the Périphérique, following signs to Genève. Leave the motorway at exit 6, and reach Pérouges via La Valbonne and Méximieux (around 45 minutes altogether). You can park by the church. ❶ Make sure you take comfortable walking shoes, as the streets are all pebbled.

SIGHTS & ATTRACTIONS

The main attraction of Pérouges is simply wandering around the village itself. You enter through a gateway, the Porte d'en Haut (the Upper Gate, the only remaining part of the 12th-century castle), past the remnant of a 15th-century gate. The **Office de Tourisme** (tourist office ❶ 04 74 46 70 84 ❾ www.perouges.org) is located at the entrance to the village.

PERFECT PÉROUGES

Its perfect look today (apart from the odd car, there are few visible signs of modernity) belies the fact that it was semi-derelict at the beginning of the 20th century. It had only a handful of inhabitants and was in danger of being demolished. Though today it still has only 73 full-time inhabitants for its 200 houses, it has undergone steady and careful restoration since 1911. The village is built almost entirely of pebbles (from the local rivers) and bricks, as stone was in short supply, and was only used to support doors, windows and the corners of houses. The success of its restoration has meant not only that it attracts many visitors, particularly during the summer, but also that it has often been used as a period location for TV and films, including *The Three Musketeers*.

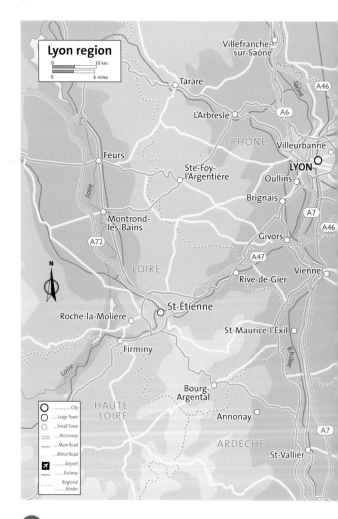

Église St-Marie-Madeleine (Church of St Mary Magdalene)

The simple and peaceful 15th-century church down a passageway next to the gate is the Église St-Marie-Madeleine. It once formed part of the village's fortifications. ◐ 08.00–20.00 (unless you have come to worship, do not enter during services)

Place du Tilleul

You should eventually reach the attractive main square, place du Tilleul (also known as place de la Halle since it once housed the covered market). The lime tree, known as the 'Tree of Liberty', in the middle of the square was planted in 1792 during the Revolution. Running around the place du Tilleul is the circular rue des Rondes, from which all streets eventually lead to the main square. Walk along rue des Rondes and you will reach the Porte d'en Bas (Lower Gate) with its inscription commemorating the siege of 1468. There is a music festival in the village from mid-May to mid-June, and a Christmas market in the place du Tilleul.

CULTURE

Musée du Vieux Pérouges (Museum of Old Pérouges)

Overseen by the Ostellerie (see page 110), the museum is a late 14th- and early 15th-century building, once belonging to the Dukes of Savoy, who used it as a hunting lodge. There is a great view of the surrounding area from the tower. You can also visit the mock-medieval garden, which was designed in the 1960s in period style. The museum contains a couple of old looms, photographs of the restoration of the village, and a few pieces of old furniture. Unfortunately, some of the best furniture was stolen a few

◆ The Church of St Mary Magdalene

⬥ *The Musée du Vieux Pérouges*

years ago. ⓐ Rue des Princes ⓣ 04 74 61 00 88 ⓛ 10.00–12.00, 14.00–17.00 daily (Easter–Sept); 10.00–12.00, 1400–17.00 Sat & Sun (Oct) ⓘ Admission charge

RETAIL THERAPY

Pérouges doesn't offer any exciting shopping experiences, but there are a few pleasant shops, mostly offering an eclectic range of goods and souvenirs. They are nearly all on rue des Rondes, which doesn't have street numbers.

Boulangerie (Didier Rapaud) An artisanal bakery with an old oven. Sells bread and galettes. ⓐ Rue des Rondes ⓣ 04 74 61 39 81 ⓛ Opening times depend on season. Wed–Mon

Caveau St-Vincent This local wine shop sells pottery, jams, carafes and glasses as well as wine, including the sweet medieval-style Hypocras. You can also have a drink and some charcuterie downstairs. ⓐ Rue des Rondes ⓣ 04 74 61 19 39 ⓛ 09.30–19.00 daily (May–Aug); 10.30–13.00, 14.30–19.00 Sat & Sun (Sept–Apr)

L'Estanco Difficult to define: a tobacconist also selling souvenirs, swords, shields, 'medieval' clothing, wine and beer. ⓐ Rue des Rondes ⓣ 04 74 61 07 20 ⓛ 10.00–12.00, 14.00–18.00 daily (May–Oct); 10.00–12.00, 14.00–18.00 Thur–Sun (Nov–Apr)

Légendes et Créations An assortment of historical costumes, dresses and craft items. ⓐ Rue du For ⓣ 04 74 37 03 97

ⓦ www.legendesetcreations.fr ⓛ 10.00–1200, 14.00–17.00 daily (summer); Sat & Sun (spring or autumn)

TAKING A BREAK

Le Relais de la Tour £ You walk in to be greeted by a suit of armour. You can get drinks, ice cream, galettes, salads or fuller meals (only served 12.00–15.00). Enter into the spirit and try some Hypocras medieval-style wine. There are tables on the square in summer. ⓐ Pl. du Tilleul ⓣ 04 74 61 01 03 ⓛ 10.00–20.00 daily

AFTER DARK

RESTAURANTS
Note that restaurant opening varies considerably according to the season. Most are open at weekends.

Auberge du Coq £ Regional cuisine, pizzas and excellent galettes (normally washed down with cider). ⓐ Rue des Rondes ⓣ 04 74 61 05 47 ⓛ 12.30–14.30, 18.00–21.30 Tues–Sat, 12.30–14.30 Sun

Le Veneur Noir £–££ A bar and restaurant with a terrace. Specialises in meat cooked on hot stones. ⓐ At the entrance of the village ⓣ 04 74 61 07 06 ⓛ 12.00–13.30, 19.30–21.30 Thur–Tues

Ostellerie du Vieux Pérouges ££–£££ There has been an inn on this site since the 14th century, though the present building

◆ *Dine at the charming Ostellerie du Vieux Pérouges*

dates from the 18th century, and was restored in 1912. The price symbol applies to the restaurant; the Ostellerie also has a more casual tea room for snacks. The restaurant draws people from around the area for its excellent local cuisine and fish. It even attracted Bill Clinton in 1996. The waitresses wear white caps and pinafores, and the wine list is written on parchment.
ⓐ Pl. du Tilleul ⓣ 04 74 61 00 88 ⓛ 12.00–14.00, 19.00–22.00

ACCOMMODATION

If you want to stay in medieval Pérouges itself, the options are:

Le Grenier à Sel £ This newly opened five-room B&B is charming and quiet and has fine views of the surrounding countryside.
ⓐ Rue des Rondes ⓣ 04 74 46 71 90 ⓦ www.hebergement-perouges.fr

Casa la Signora di Perugia ££–£££ Stylish, if expensive, *chambre d'hôte*, with a terrace and two small pools. The five suites are all decorated according to historical themes. ⓐ Porte d'en Bas
ⓣ 04 74 61 47 03 ⓦ www.casaperugia.com

Hostellerie de Pérouges ££–£££ Rates vary depending on whether you stay in the main building (more expensive) or another one on the main square. The hotel has 28 comfortable rooms. ⓐ Pl. du Tilleul ⓣ 04 74 61 00 88 ⓦ www.hostelleriedeperouges.com

Vienne

Designated one of the 120 'Towns of Art and History' by France's Ministry of Culture, you'll see why once you start walking around Vienne's historic centre. The narrow streets, pleasant squares and a mixture of architecture – from the Roman period onwards – are barely matched by other French towns of its size. A day trip is easily enough to squeeze in all the main sights.

Vienne has been inhabited since the 3rd century BC (originally by a group of Gauls called the Allobroges) and became a Roman colony in around AD 40. The town developed along both banks of the Rhône and became one of the largest settlements in Gaul. Evidence of its importance in Roman times is visible throughout the town today. Vienne later became an important centre of Christianity, coming under the rule of the Burgundians in the late 5th century. In the 11th century, the town became part of the Holy Roman Empire, and then part of the kingdom of France in 1450. But its fortunes declined as it was gradually overshadowed by Lyon.

There was an economic revival in the late 18th century, thanks to the establishment of textile factories and metallurgical works along the River Gère, to the north of the Old Town, and the population grew as a result. However, by the mid-20th century, the textile industry had largely disappeared in the face of competition. Today, Vienne, with a population of 30,000, is the home of service businesses, with some high-tech industries. Two bridges, one a footbridge, cross over to the west bank of the Rhône.

GETTING THERE

It's easy to get to Vienne from Lyon by train (from either Perrache or Part-Dieu station) – the journey time is 20–30 minutes. The train station is next to the Old Town. If you want to drive from Lyon, take the A7, following signs to Marseille and then to Vienne itself. It should take 30–35 minutes.

SIGHTS & ATTRACTIONS

Head down either rue Boson or the attractive cours Romestang (both come off cours Brillier) to get into the heart of the Old Town. If you go down rue Boson, you will pass the church of St-Pierre and its archaeological museum. Both rue Boson and cours Romestang will also lead you to the Cathédrale St-Maurice and – to the east of it – the place de Miremont, which houses the Musée des Beaux-Arts & d'Archéologie (see page 119). A little farther north, and you will get to the place Charles de Gaulle, and the temple of the former Roman forum. There are cafés outside the temple, from which you can admire it. The tower you will see to the right was once part of a palace, and dates from the 16th century. Heading down the pedestrianised rue des Clercs, you will reach the church of St-André le Bas (see page 117), with its immensely attractive cloisters, which overlooks the Rhône.

You should also try to find time to cross the Rhône to have a look at the museum and site of St-Romain-en-Gaul. If you can, take the ten-minute walk along cours de Verdun, south of cours Brillier (which has a small park coming off it near the tourist

⬤ *You can't miss Vienne's Roman Pyramide*

office) and take a look at Vienne's famous Pyramide, once the centrepiece of the Roman circus, where chariot races took place. You might also be tempted to have a drink at the Pyramide hotel (see pages 123 & 124), one of France's most famous temples of gastronomy.

At the start of your visit, you can get an audio guide from the tourist office (see box below) and follow the path marked by plaques on the ground. You can also get a combined museum ticket costing around €6.

Cathédrale St-Maurice (Cathedral of St Maurice)

The dark and imposing cathedral (a parish church since 1790) was built between the late 11th and the early 16th centuries. The exterior, which is being slowly restored, is Gothic, though the interior is a mixture of Romanesque and Gothic styles. There had been an earlier cathedral on the site since the 4th or 5th century. There are carvings of biblical scenes throughout, and intriguing zodiac carvings in the choir. Some of the masonry

JAZZ IT UP

The main event in Vienne is its well-known jazz festival (Jazz à Vienne), which takes place from late June to mid-July around town, but particularly in the Roman theatre (see page 120). Details and tickets are available from the tourist office (❸ Cours Brillier (just by the Rhône) ❶ 04 74 53 80 30 Ⓦ www.vienne-tourisme.com). There is also a fête in mid-June.

🔺 *The striking interior of the Cathédrale St-Maurice*

used in the cathedral's construction is actually Roman in origin.
ⓐ Pl. St-Paul ⓦ http://cathedraledevienne.com ⓛ 08.30–18.00

Église & Cloître St-André le Bas (Church & Cloister of St-André le Bas)

Once part of an important abbey founded in the 6th century,
the church was substantially rebuilt in the 11th and 12th centuries.
It is notable for its Romanesque ornamentation. Unfortunately,
you can't visit it without a guide. You can, however, visit the very
pleasing 12th-century cloister, in which several of the pillars are
differently decorated. The building adjoining the cloister houses
temporary art exhibitions. ⓐ Pl. du Jeu-de-Paume ⓣ 04 74 85 18 49

🕐 09.30–13.00, 14.00–18.00 Tues–Sun (Apr–Oct); 09.30–12.30, 14.00–17.00 Mon–Fri, 13.30–17.30 Sat & Sun (Nov–Mar)
❶ Admission charge (except first Sun each month)

Jardin Archéologique de Cybèle (Archaeological Garden)

These Roman ruins, now essentially a park, as well as a venue during the Jazz Festival (see page 116), were properly excavated when the hospital standing on the site was knocked down. One side of the site formed part of the forum, and is thought to have contained baths and a small theatre or odeon. It is also a good place to have a picnic. Nearby is place du Pilori, where you will find a timber-framed medieval house. ⓐ Rue des Orfèvres

Temple d'Auguste & de Livie (Temple of Augustus & Livia)

Originally built around 20–10 BC, the temple (the centre of the Roman forum) was dedicated to Roman emperors, Augustus in particular, during whose reign it was constructed. In the early Middle Ages (probably 6th century) it became a church with walls between the columns – a fact that helped to preserve it. It was restored in the late 19th century. You can't actually enter it without a guide (book through the tourist office, whose staff will advise on opening times). ⓐ Pl. Charles de Gaulle

CULTURE

Musée Archéologique & Église St-Pierre (Archaeological Museum & Church of St Peter)

Dating from the 5th or 6th century, this church is one of the oldest in France, configured as a basilica. The belfry was built in the 12th century. Since 1872 it has housed an archaeological museum, which includes ancient Gallo-Roman sculptures, masonry and mosaics. ❷ Pl. St-Pierre ❶ 04 74 85 20 35 ❹ 09.30–13.00, 14.00–18.00 Tues–Sun (Apr–Oct); 09.30–12.30, 14.00–17.00 Tues–Fri, 14.00–18.00 Sat & Sun (Nov–Mar) ❶ Admission charge (except first Sun each month)

Musée des Beaux-Arts & d'Archéologie (Fine Arts & Archaeological Museum)

Rather old-fashioned, and not the most inspiring museum you will come across, but the first floor houses a collection of local Gallic and Gallo-Roman artefacts (including some fine silverware), as well as 18th-century earthenware and 16th- to 19th-century works by local artists. The building, a former grain market, was built in the early 19th century, and is set in the centre of the square. Temporary exhibitions, and events such as arts and crafts fairs, and a Christmas market are held on the ground floor. ❷ Pl. de Miremont ❶ 04 74 85 50 42 ❹ 09.30–13.00, 14.00–18.00 Tues–Sun (Apr–Oct); 09.30–12.30, 14.00–17.00 Tues–Fri, 14.00–18.00 Sat & Sun (Nov–Mar) ❶ Admission charge (except first Sun each month)

Musée de Saint-Romain-en-Gal (Saint-Romain-en-Gal Museum)

On the west bank of the Rhône just beyond the road bridge, the archaeological site was a district of Roman Vienne, dating from the 1st century AD, and full of workshops, shops and warehouses in ancient times. The 7-hectare (17-acre) site began to be excavated in the late 1960s. You can wander around it, and get some idea of how the Romans lived. It also has two picnic areas.

The ultra-modern steel and glass museum – from which you can see the site – opened in 1996. The well-laid-out displays and models, including murals and some stunning mosaics, are designed to illustrate Roman daily life. There are great views of the Rhône and Vienne, particularly from the brasserie. ❸ Route départementale 502 ☏ 04 74 53 74 01 Ⓦ www.musees-gallo-romains.com 🕐 10.00–18.00 Tues–Sun ❶ Admission charge (except Thur)

Théâtre Romain (Roman Theatre)

Likely to have been built in around AD 40–50 into the side of a hill, this is one of the largest remaining theatres of the Roman world. It is 130 m (427 ft) in diameter, and was once capable of

⬤ The Théâtre Romain is now a music concert venue

holding 13,000 spectators. Excavation and restoration took from 1923 to 1938. It is now the main venue for the Jazz Festival (see page 116), as well as being used for rock concerts and other musical events. If you enjoy a degree of comfort, take a cushion. ⓐ Rue du Cirque ⓣ 04 74 85 39 23 ⓛ 09.30–13.00, 14.00–18.00 daily (Apr–Aug); 09.30–13.00, 14.00–18.00 Tues–Sun (Sept & Oct); 09.30–12.00, 14.00–17.00 Tues–Fri, 13.30–17.30 Sat & Sun (Nov–Mar) ⓘ Admission charge (except first Sun each month)

RETAIL THERAPY

There are several interesting shops near the main sights, particularly in rue Joseph Brenier and rue Marchande. You will also find plenty of shops, including chain stores, pharmacies and banks, around the place de Miremont. There is an excellent market in place François Mitterand on weekday mornings, but nothing to rival the huge market – one of the biggest in France – that covers much of the Old Town on Saturday mornings.

Boutique Patrick Henriroux The shop of the Pyramide hotel and restaurant (see pages 123 & 124) sells wine, kitchen equipment, spices, sauces, mustards, crockery and other culinary items. ⓐ 14 blvd Fernand Point ⓣ 04 74 53 01 96 ⓛ 09.00–12.00, 14.30–19.30 Mon & Thur–Sat, 09.00–12.30, 14.30–18.00 Sun

Carréblanc Part of the French chain selling brightly coloured and interestingly patterned bedlinen, bathrobes, towels and other household items. ⓐ 26 rue Joseph Brenier ⓣ 04 74 31 70 98 ⓛ 09.00–18.00 Tues–Sat

Le Cellier One of Vienne's best wine shops, with a very good selection of local wines from the Rhône Valley. ⓐ 50 rue Joseph Brenier ⓣ 04 74 85 40 81 ⓛ 09.00–18.00 Tues–Sat

La Gâterie One of the few traditional patisseries left in Vienne, it produces delicious pastries, cakes, biscuits and confectionery. ⓐ 22 rue de la Juiverie ⓣ 04 74 85 32 59 ⓛ 08.30–18.30 Tues–Sat

Natalys Fun and high-quality children's clothing. ⓐ 69 rue Marchande ⓣ 04 74 78 18 57 ⓛ 09.00–18.30 Tues–Sat

Sia Candles, glass and decorative household objects. ⓐ 25 rue Joseph Brenier ⓣ 04 74 85 18 94 ⓛ 09.00–18.30

TAKING A BREAK

Le Café des Orfèvres £ Straightforward traditional food, renowned for its big salads. ⓐ 31 rue des Orfèvres ⓣ 04 74 31 97 70 ⓛ 11.00–14.00, 17.00–23.00 Mon–Sat

Le Verre en l'Air £ For drinks and simple meals. ⓐ 14 rue Henry Jacquier ⓣ 04 74 78 01 43 ⓛ 10.00–16.00, 18.00–23.00

AFTER DARK

RESTAURANTS
La Chamade £–££ Right in the heart of the Old Town, a small and simple place with white walls, serving traditional dishes

such as snails and *andouillette* (local tripe sausage) at reasonable prices. ⓐ 24 rue de la Juiverie ⓣ 04 74 85 30 34 ⓛ 12.00–15.00, 19.00–22.00

Ma Grand-Mère £–££ Salads, Lyonnais specialities and very good steaks. ⓐ 8 rue du Musée ⓣ 04 74 31 61 84 ⓛ 12.00–13.30, 19.30–21.30 Thur–Mon

Le Bec Fin ££ Near the cathedral, serving high-quality local specialities as well as dishes from other parts of France. ⓐ 7 pl. St-Maurice ⓣ 04 74 85 76 72 ⓛ 11.00–15.00, 19.00–23.00

Le Cloître ££ One of Vienne's best restaurants. Set on two floors. ⓐ 2 rue des Cloîtres ⓣ 04 74 31 93 57 ⓦ www.le-cloitre.net ⓛ 12.00–15.00, 19.30–21.00 Mon–Fri

La Pyramide £££ Founded by the legendary Fernand Point, this is one of the most famous restaurants in France. The food is superb – imaginative, light and modern, with intense flavours. The owner and chef, Patrick Henriroux, actually cooks there (unusual these days) and personally goes to the market every morning to choose his produce. The prices of the set menus are very good value for the quality, though they're steep if you choose from the à la carte menu. Local wines are sensibly priced. There's a children's menu, and the service is friendly and efficient. Many locals go there. You can eat in the pretty garden in summer. ⓐ 14 blvd Fernand Point ⓣ 04 74 53 01 96 ⓛ 12.00–14.00, 19.30–21.30 Thur–Mon

BARS

Bar du Temple Right in front of the Roman temple, this bar is a popular and friendly meeting place. Outdoor seating in summer. ⓐ 5 pl. Charles de Gaulle ① 04 74 31 94 19 ⓛ 07.00–24.00 daily (summer); 07.00–24.00 Mon–Sat (winter)

Pub 38 A lively bar that serves beer, cocktails and ice creams (snacks are also available). Good for a late drink. ⓐ 5 rue Voltaire ① 04 37 02 08 74 ⓛ 12.00–24.00 Mon–Sat, closed Sun

ACCOMMODATION

Grand Hôtel de la Poste £ Basic, but a good budget choice. Located in the Old Town. ⓐ 47 cours Romestang ① 04 74 95 02 04 ⓦ www.hotel-vienne.fr

La Pyramide £££ *The* hotel in Vienne – and one of the best in the area – famous now for decades, with a guest list including the Duke and Duchess of Windsor, Clark Gable and Rita Hayworth (to name but a few). Stars of the jazz festival (see page 116) also stay there. The rooms are extremely well appointed, and the buffet breakfasts unusual and memorable. ⓐ 14 blvd Fernand Point ① 04 74 53 01 96 ⓦ www.lapyramide.com

◗ *Waiting for the funicular*

PRACTICAL
information

Directory

GETTING THERE

By air

British Airways flies direct from the UK to Lyon, with regular flights from Heathrow. EasyJet also flies there, from Stansted. Flights can often be very reasonably priced if you book well in advance. Other airlines, including Air France, fly there indirectly, but these flights take much longer. Flying British Airways from Heathrow takes around 1 hour and 45 minutes.

British Airways ☎ 0844 493 0787 ⓦ www.ba.com
easyJet ☎ 0871 244 2366 ⓦ www.easyjet.com
Lyon St-Exupéry International Airport ☎ 04 26 06 70 67
ⓦ www.lyonaeroports.com

Many people are aware that air travel emits CO_2, which contributes to climate change. You may be interested in the possibility of lessening the environmental impact of your flight through the charity **Climate Care** (ⓦ www.jpmorganclimatecare.com), which offsets your CO_2 by funding environmental projects around the world.

By rail

From London you can get to Lyon by Eurostar, leaving from **St Pancras International** (ⓦ www.stpancras.com), changing for a TGV at either Paris – where you have to transfer from the Gare du Nord to the Gare de Lyon – or Lille. Trains going via Lille stop at Lyon Part-Dieu station, and usually have a slightly shorter journey time since you will need to allow around an hour to transfer between the two Paris stations. Some trains from Paris also stop at Lyon Perrache station. The total journey time via Paris is around $5^{1}/_{2}$ hours. The best way to book is through Rail Europe.

Eurostar reservations (UK) ⓘ 08432 186 186
ⓦ www.eurostar.com

French Railways (SNCF) ⓦ www.sncf.com

Rail Europe ⓘ 0844 848 4070 ⓦ www.raileurope.co.uk

The monthly *Thomas Cook European Rail Timetable* has up-to-date schedules for European international and national train services. **Thomas Cook European Rail Timetable** ⓘ (UK) 01733 416477, (USA) 1 800 322 3834 ⓦ www.thomascookpublishing.com

By road

There are several routes you can take to get to Lyon from Calais. Either you can take the A26, the A1 and A3 and go via the outskirts

⬤ *International flights arrive at the modern St-Exupéry airport*

of Paris, ending up on the A6, or you can skirt around Paris, and eventually join the A6 further south. Remember to have euros or a credit card with you to pay for toll roads. The distance from Calais is around 750 km (466 miles), and it should take you 6–7 hours. The driving time from Paris is around 4 hours. The quickest way to cross the Channel with a car is by Eurotunnel, although there are also several ferry companies to choose from.

Eurotunnel ☎ 08705 35 35 35 Ⓦ www.eurotunnel.com
For route map: Ⓦ www.rac.co.uk

ENTRY FORMALITIES
Passports are needed by UK visitors and all others except EU citizens who can produce a national identity card. Visits of up to three months do not require a visa if you are from the EU, USA, Canada, Australia or New Zealand. Other travellers should consult the French embassy, consulate or tourist office in their own country about visa requirements. Ⓦ www.diplomatie.gouv.fr

Residents of the UK, Ireland and other EU countries may bring into France personal possessions and goods for personal use, including a reasonable amount of tobacco and alcohol, provided they have been bought in the EU. There are few formalities at the points of entry into France. Residents of non-EU countries, and EU residents arriving from a non-EU country, may bring in up to 400 cigarettes and 50 cigars or 50 g (2 oz) tobacco; 2 litres (3 bottles) of wine and 1 litre (approx 2 pints) of spirits and liqueurs.

MONEY
The euro (€) is the official currency in France. €1 = 100 cents. It comes in notes of €5, €10, €20, €50, €100, €200 and €500.

Coins are in denominations of €1 and €2, and 1, 2, 5, 10, 20 and 50 cents.

ATMs can be found at the airport, railway stations and all over the city. They accept most British and international debit and credit cards. They are the quickest and most convenient way (and often the cheapest) to obtain cash. Instructions are usually available in English and other major European languages.

Credit cards are almost universally accepted except occasionally at smaller shops, cafés and markets. You will have to know your PIN, as the chip-and-PIN system is normally used in France. Note that some shops and other establishments have a minimum spend policy, so won't accept cards below a certain limit. VISA is the most frequently accepted card. You will have no difficulty in finding banks and bureaux de change.

HEALTH, SAFETY & CRIME

It is safe to drink tap water, as most people do, although some prefer to drink mineral water. There are no major precautions you need to take when eating local food and, on the whole, you need worry no more than at home.

Medical care in France is of a very high standard, but expensive unless you have suitable travel insurance. Most minor ailments can be dealt with at pharmacies – of which there are many – indicated by green cross signs. The staff are qualified to offer medical advice and dispense a wide range of medicines.

Lyon is generally safe, but as in all large cities, you should be careful late at night. Otherwise, you should take sensible precautions – particularly in crowded places or at tables outside in restaurants – such as keeping your bag or camera close to you.

TRAVEL INSURANCE

Visitors from the UK are covered by EU reciprocal health schemes while in France. They require a European Health Insurance Card (EHIC). This will not cover all possible expenses, and only guarantees emergency treatment. You can apply for this online from the **UK Department of Health** (Ⓦ www.dh.gov.uk). Always make sure you have adequate travel insurance, covering not only health, but possessions and baggage, etc. All non-EU travellers should make sure they have adequate insurance before they travel.

In general, the police try to be helpful, but may not speak English. There are three main types of police: the Police Municipale are the ones you are most likely to see overseeing traffic and petty crime, including lost property, in towns; the Police Nationale deal with more serious matters in larger towns; while in country districts and on motorways, the Gendarmerie Nationale, a military force, is the main law enforcement body.

If you are robbed, you should make a statement at your nearest police station to make an insurance claim.

OPENING HOURS

Shops open 09.00 or 10.00–19.00 or 19.30 Monday to Saturday, though some smaller shops open 09.00–12.00, 14.00–19.00. But most shops in tourist areas (such as Vieux Lyon) are normally open all day, and on Sunday, and close later; and bakeries, for instance, open earlier. Some shops are closed on Monday.

Markets usually open at 08.00 or 09.00 (sometimes earlier for food markets) and start packing up around 12.30. Antiques, clothes and bric-a-brac markets often close later.

Office hours are usually 08.30–12.00, 14.00–18.00 Monday to Friday. They also close on public holidays.

Banks open 08.30–12.00, 13.30–17.00 Monday to Friday, though times may vary slightly, with some banks open all day, for instance, and others opening later or closing earlier. They are closed on public holidays, and close earlier the day before. So your best bet is to get there mid-morning.

Museum and attraction opening times vary, but they are normally open 10.00–18.00 or 19.00 in summer. However, some (usually smaller museums) close for lunch, and most have shorter hours outside the high season. Some also close on public holidays, and on either Monday or Tuesday. Entrance to bigger museums sometimes ends 30 minutes before closing, so always check before you head to them.

TOILETS

You should have no difficulty in finding a toilet. Public buildings, such as museums, usually have clean and modern toilets in the publicly accessible areas near the entrance. Many of Lyon's car parks and metro stations also have toilets. But the fastest and easiest solution is to step into a bar or café and have a quick drink there. There are also public toilets (often modern coin-operated cubicles) on the streets. In Presqu'île, you'll find public toilets in place des Jacobins and place Bellecour; in Croix-Rousse, in place Sathonay and boulevard de la Croix-Rousse; and in Vieux Lyon in rue St-Georges. In Fourvière, they are in place de Fourvière.

At the airport, train stations, and in many other public toilets, you may have to pay a small fee (normally €0.50).

CHILDREN

Children are generally welcome in France, and Lyon is no exception. The majority of hotels will normally be very helpful if you are travelling with small children. Most restaurants – particularly cafés and brasseries – gladly serve them. Indeed, many simpler places, and some very grand ones, offer children's menus (*menu enfant*). It is perfectly normal to see well-behaved teenagers, although not infants, eating in posh restaurants. Despite being the foodie capital of France, there is still plenty of food on sale that will appeal to kids.

Young children might also be amused by Lyon's painted walls, a cruise along the Saône or Rhône, the Fourvière adventure park (see page 65), the Miniatures Museum (see page 67), the Guignol puppet theatre (see page 66) or the free **zoo** (ⓐ access from blvd de Brotteaux ❶ 04 78 89 02 03 ❷ 09.30–18.30 daily (mid-Apr–mid-Oct); 09.30–16.30 daily (mid-Oct–mid-Apr) ❿ Metro: Masséna) in Parc de la Tête d'Or on the east bank of the Rhône).

There is also an **Aquarium** (ⓐ 7 rue Stephane Dechant ❶ 04 72 66 65 66 ⓦ www.aquariumlyon.fr ❷ 10.00–19.00 daily (July); 11.00–19.00 daily (Sept–June) ❿ Buses: 8, 10, 14 and 17 to Bastero on the west bank of the Saône).

COMMUNICATIONS
Internet

As it's a major business and university city, Internet access is widespread in Lyon, with Internet cafés easily found (check for addresses with your hotel or local tourist office). All but the simplest hotels provide Internet connections.

Phone

You can buy phonecards (*télécartes*) at *tabacs* (newsagents/ tobacconists sporting a red diamond sign outside), post offices and some cafés and railway stations. Some public phones also accept credit cards. Insert the card after lifting the receiver. You can also make follow-on calls.

Local directory enquiries 🛈 12
International operator 🛈 00 33 12 + country code
Freephone numbers start with 0800

TELEPHONING FRANCE

The telephone code for the area is 04, followed by an 8-digit number. When calling from anywhere in France (including Lyon), dial all 10 digits, including the 04. To dial the area from outside France, dial your own international prefix (00 in most countries) followed by 33 4, then the 8-digit local code.

TELEPHONING ABROAD

Dial 00 for an international connection, followed by your country code (UK 44, Republic of Ireland 353, USA and Canada 1, Australia 61, New Zealand 64, South Africa 27), then the area code (leaving out the first 0 if there is one) and the number. Card-operated public phone booths are everywhere, and you can make international calls from them.

Post

Post offices can be found throughout the city. Main offices open 08.00–19.00 Monday to Friday, 08.00–12.00 Saturday. The biggest one is on place A Poncet, next to place Bellecour, by the Rhône. Smaller offices open 09.00–19.00 on weekdays (some closing 12.00–14.00), and are closed Saturday afternoons. All post offices are closed on Sunday and on public holidays. You can also buy stamps in *tabacs*. The postal service is efficient, and postcards to the UK and Ireland will normally arrive in 2–3 days, taking a little longer to non-European destinations.

The current rate for sending postcards to Europe is €0.65, and for North America, Australia and New Zealand it is €0.90.

ELECTRICITY

France runs on 220 V with 2-pin plugs. British appliances will need a simple adaptor, best obtained from UK electrical shops, or at the Eurostar station or airport. You should also be able to find shops in Lyon selling adaptors. US and other equipment designed for 110 V will normally need a transformer.

TRAVELLERS WITH DISABILITIES

Lyon is generally pretty well adapted to those with disabilities. Many metro stations have lifts down to the platforms (train doors are flush with the platforms), and buses and trams also have access, as do many museums, hotels and restaurants. There are also several pedestrianised streets. The only serious problems might arise in Vieux Lyon, and climbing the slopes of Croix-Rousse (though several of the stairs have ramps). There is also special transport available (check with the tourist office).

Useful organisations for advice and information include:

Association de Paralysés de France Provides information for the whole of France. ⓐ 17 blvd Auguste Blanqui, 75013 Paris ⓣ 01 40 78 69 00 ⓦ www.apf.asso.fr

RADAR The principal UK forum and pressure group for people with disabilities. ⓐ 12 City Forum, 250 City Road, London EC1V 8AF ⓣ 020 7250 3222 ⓦ www.radar.org.uk

SATH (Society for Accessible Travel & Hospitality) Advises US-based travellers with disabilities. ⓐ 347 Fifth Ave, Suite 610, New York, NY 10016 ⓣ 212 447 7284 ⓦ www.sath.org

TOURIST INFORMATION

The city's **tourist office** is very helpful. ⓐ Office du Tourisme, pl. Bellecour ⓣ 04 72 77 69 69 ⓦ www.lyon-france.com ⓛ 09.00–18.00 daily, closed public holidays

Other useful websites are:

ⓦ www.lyon.fr (town hall site)

ⓦ www.rhonealpes-tourisme.com (the regional site)

ⓦ http://uk.franceguide.com (the French tourist board site)

Emergencies

EMERGENCY NUMBERS

The following are all free national emergency numbers:

Medical/ambulance (SAMU) ❶ 15

Police ❶ 17

Fire (Sapeurs-Pompiers) ❶ 18

Any emergency service ❶ 112. This is also the number that must be used when calling from mobile phones.

MEDICAL SERVICES

Lyon is very well supplied by high-quality medical services.

Doctors

Maisons Médicales de Gardes They will tell you who to visit near your hotel. ❶ 04 72 33 00 33

Médecins du Monde ❶ 04 78 29 59 14

SOS Medecins For emergencies, 24 hours a day, every day. ❶ 04 78 83 51 51

Dental emergencies ❶ 04 72 10 01 01

Hospitals

Croix-Rousse Hospital ❷ 103 grande rue de la Croix-Rousse ❶ 08 20 08 20 69 ❾ www.chu-lyon.fr

Hôtel Dieu Hospital ❷ 1 pl. de l'Hôpital ❶ 08 20 08 20 69

24-hour pharmacies

Pharmacie Blanchet ❷ 5 pl. des Cordeliers ❶ 04 78 42 12 42

Pharmacie Duquesne ❷ 36 rue Duquesne ❶ 04 78 93 70 96

EMERGENCY PHRASES

Help!	**Fire!**	**Stop!**
Au secours!	Au feu!	Stop!
Ossercoor!	*Oh fur!*	*Stop!*

Call an ambulance/a doctor/the police/the fire service!
Appelez une ambulance/un médecin/la police/les pompiers!
*Apperleh ewn ahngbewlahngss/uhn medesang/lah poleess/
leh pompeeyeh!*

POLICE

Central Police Station On the east bank of the Rhône.
🅐 Hôtel de Police, 40 rue Maurice Berliet 📞 04 78 78 40 40

EMBASSIES & CONSULATES

Australian Embassy 🅐 4 rue Jean Ray, Paris 📞 01 40 59 33 00
Canadian Consulate 🅐 17 rue Bourgelat, Lyon 📞 04 72 77 64 07
Irish Embassy 🅐 4 rue Rude, Paris 📞 01 44 17 67 00
New Zealand Embassy 🅐 7 rue Léonard da Vinci, Paris
📞 01 45 01 43 43
South African Embassy 🅐 59 quai d'Orsay, Paris 📞 01 53 59 23 23
United Kingdom Consulate 🅐 24 rue Childebert, Lyon
📞 04 72 77 81 70
United States Consulate 🅐 1 quai Jules Courmont, Lyon
📞 04 78 38 36 88

ACKNOWLEDGEMENTS

The publishers would like to thank the following individuals and organisations for supplying their copyright photographs for this book: Alamy, page 57; Dreamstime (Pierre Durieu), page 107; Pictures Colour Library, pages 17, 32, 47, 93 & 127; Nicolas Rigaud/Visitors' Bureau of Lyon, page 13; World Pictures, pages 7 & 62; Anwer Bati, all others.

Project editor: Tom Willsher
Layout: Paul Queripel
Proofreaders: Karolin Thomas & Jan McCann

The author would like to thank Marine Guy, Natasha Rhymes, Amanda Monroe and Isabelle Faure for their help.

Send your thoughts to
books@thomascook.com

- Found a great bar, club, shop or must-see sight that we don't feature?
- Like to tip us off about any information that needs a little updating?
- Want to tell us what you love about this handy little guidebook and more importantly how we can make it even handier?

Then here's your chance to tell all! Send us ideas, discoveries and recommendations today and then look out for your valuable input in the next edition of this title.

Email the above address (stating the title) or write to:
pocket guides Series Editor, Thomas Cook Publishing, PO Box 227, Coningsby Road, Peterborough PE3 8SB, UK.

WHAT'S IN YOUR GUIDEBOOK?

Independent authors Impartial up-to-date information from our travel experts who meticulously source local knowledge.

Experience Thomas Cook's 165 years in the travel industry and guidebook publishing enriches every word with expertise you can trust.

Travel know-how Thomas Cook has thousands of staff working around the globe, all living and breathing travel.

Editors Travel-publishing professionals, pulling everything together to craft a perfect blend of words, pictures, maps and design.

You, the traveller We deliver a practical, no-nonsense approach to information, geared to how you really use it.

Useful phrases

English	French	Approx pronunciation
BASICS		
Yes	Oui	*Wee*
No	Non	*Nawng*
Please	S'il vous plaît	*Sylvooplay*
Thank you	Merci	*Mehrsee*
Hello	Bonjour	*Bawng-zhoor*
Goodbye	Au revoir	*Aw revwahr*
Excuse me	Excusez-moi	*Ekskewzeh-mwah*
Sorry	Désolé(e)	*Dehzoleh*
That's okay	Ça va	*Sa va*
I don't speak French	Je ne parle pas français	*Zher ner pahrl pah frahngsay*
Do you speak English?	Parlez-vous anglais?	*Pahrlay-voo ahnglay?*
Good morning	Bonjour	*Bawng-zhoor*
Good afternoon	Bonjour	*Bawng-zhoor*
Good evening	Bonsoir	*Bawng-swah*
Goodnight	Bonne nuit	*Bon nwee*
My name is ...	Je m'appelle ...	*Zher mahpehl ...*
NUMBERS		
One	Un/Une	*Uhn/Ewn*
Two	Deux	*Dur*
Three	Trois	*Trwah*
Four	Quatre	*Kahtr*
Five	Cinq	*Sank*
Six	Six	*Seess*
Seven	Sept	*Seht*
Eight	Huit	*Weet*
Nine	Neuf	*Nurf*
Ten	Dix	*Deess*
Twenty	Vingt	*Vang*
Fifty	Cinquante	*Sangkahnt*
One hundred	Cent	*Sohn*
SIGNS & NOTICES		
Airport	Aéroport	*Ahehrohpohr*
Rail station	Gare	*Gahr*
Platform	Quai	*Kay*
Smoking/	Permit de fumer/	*Permee der foom-eh/*
No smoking	Interdit de fumer	*Anterdee der foom-eh*
Toilets	Toilettes	*Twahlett*
Ladies/Gentlemen	Femmes/Hommes	*Fam/Ommh*
Subway/Bus	Métro/Bus	*Maytroa/Booss*